C000277274

Successful Pistol Shooting

The authors on the Century range at Bisley after Paul Leatherdale had just shot to retain his British Pistol Champion title in 1984.

SUCCESSFUL PISTOL SHOOTING

Frank and Paul Leatherdale

The Crowood Press

First published in 1988 by
The Crowood Press
Ramsbury, Marlborough,
Wiltshire SN8 2HE

© Frank Leatherdale and Paul Leatherdale 1988

All rights reserved. No part of this publication may be reproduced
or transmitted in any form or by any means, electronic or
mechanical, including photocopy, recording, or any information
storage and retrieval system, without permission in writing from
the publishers.

British Library Cataloguing in Publication Data

Leatherdale, Frank
    Successful pistol shooting.
    1. Pistol shooting——Handbooks, manuals, etc.
    I. Title II. Leatherdale, Paul
    799.3′12   GV1175

ISBN 1 85223 057 6

Typeset by Action Typesetting Limited
Imperial House, Russell Street, Gloucester
Printed in Great Britain by The Bath Press

Contents

Acknowledgements

Without the help of many people we would not have been able to write this book. In particular we would like to thank Jean Leatherdale – wife and mother respectively – for her support over many years of pistol shooting, and for her help in proof-reading our writing.

We would also like to thank Reg Cox and Peter Hicks who have so willingly helped us with the photographic illustrations and who have guided us with their professional expertise in these matters.

We also wish to record the help given by the following people or companies in providing photographs which we hope help to make this book interesting and more easily understood: Abbey Supply Company; Britarms; Reg Cox; Hammerli Ltd; Hicks Photographic Services; Noptel Ky; National Rifle Association of America; Parker-Hale Ltd; Peters Stahl; RX-Products Ltd; Viking Arms Ltd; Westlake Engineering; Lt.-Col. T.W. Whittaker.

Foreword

Anyone who wishes to take up competitive pistol shooting will find an introductory book on this topic very useful. Such a book as *Successful Pistol Shooting* was not available 32 years ago when I first started competitive pistol shooting. Since then there have been only a few books published on this subject. Most of these cover special events or topics and not the broad range of pistol shooting activities available today.

Frank Leatherdale, the domestic British

National Pistol Coach, and his son, Paul, have extensive pistol shooting experience. They have provided a detailed overview of the many different pistol shooting disciplines. The basic elements and principles of pistol shooting techniques common to all pistol shooting events are presented in a clear, logical manner which will make interesting reading for all. Information on the many different types of competitive pistols, their ammunition and equipment for the various disciplines is fully illustrated. Sections on technical, physical and psychological training for pistol shooting offer excellent groundwork for the beginner and a good review for the experienced shooter. Both domestic and international pistol shooting are carefully described.

Frank's extensive coaching experience is apparent in this book. Paul's contribution is based on his international shooting experience and first-hand information obtained from talking to many world-class pistol shooters.

Whether you are a beginner or an experienced pistol shooter, I recommend that you read this book. It provides the bases for all competitive pistol shooting. You may consider the book a road map of how you can progress from local club to national, and on to the international level of pistol shooting.

Darius R. Young

Dr Young, although living in Canada and teaching at the University of Alberta, has been on the United States International Shooting Team on twelve occasions. He has competed world-wide and has won over 100 different international shooting medals, either individually or as a member of the United States team. As a current member of the United States team (1987–88), he has competed in five World Cups, two national competitions and the Pan American Games.

Introduction

Pistol shooting is a sport which continues to gather more participants to it year by year. There are several reasons for this growth. As a sport it satisfies the aspirations of people of all ages: it requires keen mental involvement as well as a reasonably fit body. Pistol shooting presents a continual challenge to each individual; and yet, because of the way the sport is organised in classes according to ability, each person – young or old, weak or strong, male or

Mrs Eileen Cunningham shooting to win the Ladies Championship and Class C at the 1985 British Pistol Championship at Bisley.

11

Practical pistol being shot on the Short Siberia range at Bisley.

female, experienced or beginner – can shoot and compete on equal terms.

Furthermore, pistol shooting can be as exciting as you wish it to be because there are several different types of shooting, ranging from firing one shot every one and a half minutes with an air pistol, to firing five shots in four seconds with a rapid-fire pistol, or firing one shot in three seconds with a full-bore pistol. Each form presents its own intriguing challenge.

It is a sport whose competitors benefit from the comradeship of club membership, with its team competitions, and yet when you, the shooter, are facing the target, you are alone, striving to control your emotions and hopes, your fears and frustrations, your joy and elation and, above all, your excitement.

In *Successful Pistol Shooting* we have tried to give you all the information you need to help you enjoy your sport to the full, knowing that real enjoyment comes from success, at whatever level you wish to participate. We can think of no other sport where a thorough understanding of the basic principles is so important to later success. Even when you have acquired a lot of experience and skill you will still need to remember and apply the basic principles you were taught at the beginning. That is why we recommend experienced shooters to reread Chapter 2 from time to time.

HOW TO USE THIS BOOK

In Chapter 1 we tell you how to take up the sport, who you may contact, the types of shooting that are available, how to choose a pistol, and what other equipment you will need.

Chapter 2 describes the basic principles of pistol shooting, which will apply no matter which form of the sport you wish to take up. We have tried to make this part as clear and complete as possible without introducing confusing details which can best be understood later on.

In Chapter 3 we have described the international types of shooting which form the basis of the competitions in the Olympic and Commonwealth Games and in World Champion-ships, and which are widely used elsewhere. We have described how the basic principles we covered in Chapter 2 may need to be modified to embrace the specific conditions of a particular type of event.

Training and development are dealt with in Chapter 4 where we advise on the physical and mental preparation you should undertake, and how to prepare yourself for an important match. How to shoot such a match is covered in Chapter 5.

1 How to Take Up Pistol Shooting

WHO TO CONTACT

If you wish to take up the sport of pistol shooting you should join a pistol club or meet an experienced person who can tell you about the sport and facilities available in your area. Useful Addresses lists the headquarters of the various organisations responsible for different types of pistol shooting. You can write to any of these places to obtain information on whom to contact in your locality. If you have no particular inclination to try some special aspect of the sport, we would recommend that you start by learning the basic principles of pistol shooting using a small-bore pistol. This has a calibre of .22 – so your first approach will be to the National Small-bore Rifle Association in Great Britain, or to the National Rifle Association of America in the United States. (Despite their titles, both these organisations are governing bodies in their respective countries for pistol shooting and rifle shooting.)

JOINING A CLUB

The advantages of joining your local pistol club are considerable. Most clubs will have a qualified club instructor or coach who will be able to tell you the pros and cons of different techniques, and who will see that you learn the sport along well proven lines. You will be properly trained in how to handle firearms safely. Should you start to develop any bad fault it will be corrected at an early stage before it becomes a habit. Usually the club will have at least one type of pistol which you may use whilst you are learning the basic principles.

You will also be able to see other people shooting; see the types and makes of pistol they use; see the different types of target that are shot; and benefit from the companionship which exists in shooting clubs. Not the least of the benefits of club membership will be some form of insurance cover, for you, for third parties and for your equipment.

Another reason for joining a club is that the law in Great Britain permits firearms to be used only on approved ranges. You may use an air pistol in your own garden or home – which is a good reason for shooting with this type of pistol, either as an end in itself, or as a method of training for another pistol.

Most clubs charge an annual subscription, and usually also ask for a fee each time you visit the range. This latter amount is to cover the costs of lighting and heating, and helps to keep the annual subscription to a minimum. Part of your annual club subscription will probably be used to pay the club's affiliation fee to the sport's governing body, which will entitle you to some of the benefits of being an affiliated member. These may include the right to enter national competitions arranged by the governing body, as well as extra insurance cover. In addition, the club will probably be affiliated to its county or state association, bringing you similar benefits.

As well as the local, county or state, or national pistol competitions which are shot on the club's range, there are open pistol meetings organised across the country from time to time as well as national championships and other meetings which you can enter. It is a good idea to enter as many of these events as you can because at these you will meet other shooters with whom you can discuss techniques and

*The Ruger Mk II is a sturdy pistol with fixed sights. It is useful as a
club gun for beginners (shown here with slide drawn back).*

*Changing targets during the aggregate competition at the British Pistol
Championships at Bisley.*

equipment. Do not be put off by the thought that you will be a beginner and stand no chance in competition with more experienced shooters, as all shooting is done in classes, depending on ability.

Typical Classifications: United States

Master   95.00 and above
Expert   90.00 to 94.99
Sharpshooter   85.00 to 89.99
Marksman   below 85.00

Typical Classifications: Britain

Class X   93 and above
Class A   from 89 and under 93
Class B   from 85 and under 89
Class C   from 79 and under 85
Class D   under 79

SELECTING YOUR FIRST PISTOL

Pistols are quite expensive items, but if they are looked after properly they hold their value quite well and may be regarded as an investment. Unless you know exactly what type of pistol you want for your first purchase, you should look at the range of good second-hand ones available. There are usually quite a number from which to choose in your local gunshop, within your club or county association, or from your national body.

The advantage in buying a good second-hand pistol first of all is that it will save you money at the outset. You may need to take an experienced pistol shooter along with you to check the mechanical condition of your proposed purchase. If possible, try to fire it before you make your final decision. Make sure that the pistol feels right for you. You can alter the shape of the grips to suit your hand but here again an experienced shooter will be able to advise you when he sees how you hold the pistol. What you should look for is a pistol whose balance feels right for you (no two people

have the same size of hand or physique), and one which 'points' well. That is, when you bring the pistol up on aim, the foresight is centred in the notch in the rearsight, without you having to bend your wrist.

If you are buying an air pistol you will need one which is .177 calibre, recoil-less. Air pistols depreciate more quickly than other pistols; you would be well advised to shoot the pistol to see that it groups well, and that the barrel or piston has not worn. It might just need washers replacing, which can easily be done to restore the pistol to full efficiency.

OTHER ESSENTIAL EQUIPMENT

You will need other equipment apart from a pistol, some of which is essential.

Ear and Eye Protection

Pistol shooting can be harmful to your ears, as the gases are still burning when they leave the muzzle. Thus there are more noisy and harmful shock waves from pistol shooting compared with rifle shooting, even using the same ammunition, due to the pistol's shorter barrel. There are two types of ear protectors: muffs which fit over the ear and plugs which fit into the ear. Many shooters wear both together for full protection.

Your eyes should be protected from hot cartridge cases, burning debris, and fragments of lead or brass ejected from your, or someone else's, pistol. For this you will need spectacles with toughened glass in them. If you normally wear glasses with hardened lenses you are all right, if not you will need to buy a pair of shooting glasses.

Telescope and Stand

You will need to be able to see your shot holes, and as you may be shooting at 50 metres, for example, you will need a telescope with 20 × or 30 × magnification. It is annoying and tiring

DESIRABLE EQUIPMENT

Stop-watch

You will soon find that an easily read stop-watch is very useful, as so much of your shooting will be against the clock and you will need to know how time is passing.

Tools

Some tools usually come with the pistol, such as screwdrivers to fit its screws or with which to adjust the sight. You will also need a cleaning rod, with cleaning brushes and a jag for holding flannelette patches. You will need a can of thin gun oil and a can of anti-corrosive liquid.

Sight Black

We recommend a carbide-burning sight black 'lamp' (*see* Chapter 2).

Shooting Cap

A shooting cap not only shields your eyes when shooting towards the sun, or other light, but also helps to protect you from your neighbour's empty cases. Shooting caps should have long peaks and side flaps which can be held back on top of the peak if not required.

Score Book and Pen

You will find it both useful and enjoyable to maintain a record of your scores. You may well have to make up your own score book to suit your needs.

Shooting Box

By now you will have realised that it will help if you have a shooting box in which to carry all your equipment. This will keep everything together and can be laid out so that there is a place for each item. You will quickly be able to see that you have all that you need with you. It is most upsetting to arrive at a range to find you have left something vital at home. Shooting

Ears and eyes protected: in this case there is an orthoptic fitted to the shooting glasses and the left eye is screened behind an improvised shield.

trying to see a shot hole in poor light with an inadequate telescope, and this can upset your shooting. The telescope will need some form of stand which will hold it steadily at your eye level, even in a wind. Some people mount their scope in the lid of their shooting box, but this is not as flexible as having a separate stand for it.

Ammunition

Obviously you will need ammunition to suit your pistol. If you have joined a club, it is probable that you can buy ammunition at the club as and when you are going to shoot, which is all right in the beginning. Later on you will want to use ammunition from a proven batch, and will therefore want to buy your own in quantities which will give you some continuity.

boxes vary from elaborate wooden boxes, strong and large enough for you to sit on whilst waiting, to a mere cloth bag which contains your pistol, magazines and ammunition.

Rule Book

It will help you to understand the sport and to get off to a good start if you are familiar with the rules and regulations which govern it. You should have one or more of the official rule books listed in Further Reading.

Please do not be frightened or put off by the number of books listed there. You will only need one book initially and perhaps another when you develop on to UIT (Union Internationale de Tir) types of shooting.

COURSES OF FIRE

There are various types of pistol shooting which you can do, and these are known as disciplines. Each has its own course of fire. Some disciplines are shot all over the world, and others are particular to certain countries.

International Disciplines (UIT)

1. *Free pistol event*: this is shot at a distance of 50 metres and consists of 60 shots fired in two and a half hours, using .22 ammunition.
2. *Air pistol event*: this is normally shot indoors at a distance of ten metres and consists of 60 shots for men and junior men, in the space of two and a quarter hours and 40 shots for ladies and junior ladies in the space of one and a half hours.
3. *Rapid-fire event*: this is shot at a distance of 25 metres and consists of 60 shots divided into two stages of 30 shots each. Each stage is subdivided into six series of five shots each. The first two series are shot in eight seconds, the next two in six seconds and the last two in four seconds. In each series one shot is fired at each of five targets.
4. *Sport pistol and centre fire events*: the course of fire is the same in these two events, but the sport pistol is for ladies and juniors and the small-bore pistol is used. These events are shot at a distance of 25 metres. The 60-shot course of fire is divided into two stages of 30 shots each: a 'precision' stage and a 'rapid-fire' stage (previously known as duelling).
5. *Standard pistol event*: this is shot at a distance of 25 metres and consists of 60 shots divided into three stages of 20 shots each. It is shot with a small-bore pistol. The first stage consists of four series of five shots, each shot in 150 seconds (slow fire). The second stage consists of four series of five shots, each shot in 20 seconds (timed fire). The third stage consists of four series of five shots, each shot in ten seconds (rapid fire). This is both an enjoyable and useful event as it embraces some of the elements of each speed of shooting.

American Disciplines

The NRA of America's conventional pistol competition combines slow, timed and rapid fire at distances of 50 and 25 yards outdoors, or 50 feet indoors. The outdoor match usually consists of 20 shots slow fire at 50 yards, shot in four strings of five shots, allowing ten minutes per string; 20 shots timed fire in four strings of five shots, each in 20 seconds; and 20 shots rapid fire in four strings of five shots, each in ten seconds. This is followed by the national match course of ten shots slow fire at 50 yards, ten shots timed fire at 25 yards (shot in two strings of five shots, each shot in 20 seconds), and ten shots rapid fire at 25 yards (shot in two strings of five shots, each in ten seconds). The possible aggregate score is therefore 900 points for the 90-shot competition.

For the 2,700-aggregate competition the above match is repeated using three different pistols – .22 calibre, a centre-fire pistol, and a .45 calibre. Many programmes call for just one or two pistols, making an aggregate of 900 or 1,800.

Most indoor matches are fired with .22 only for a 900 total. However, some indoor matches use all calibres and shoot the full 2,700-aggregate.

British Club Shooting

Most shooting in British clubs follows either one of the UIT disciplines or one of the following:

1. *Slow-fire event*: 20 shots at a distance of 20 yards, using .22 pistols and shot in ten minutes at the PL 14 target (this is the 50-metre UIT precision target scaled down to 20 yards). This course of fire is used in many individual club or county league competitions, as well as in inter-club and inter-county matches.

2. *Six yards air pistol*: this is shot with the .177 recoil-less air pistol, at a distance of six yards, and consists of 40 shots fired at the Air 8 target (which is the ten-metre UIT target scaled down to six yards).

3. *Rapid-fire event*: this is shot with either .22 short or .22 long rifle ammunition at a distance of either ten yards or ten metres at scaled down UIT rapid-fire targets. The course of fire is usually half the UIT course, that is 30 shots, divided into six series.

4. *Centre-fire (slow-fire)*: this is shot at a distance of 25 metres or 20 yards (but not mixed in any one competition) and usually consists of ten shots in 12 minutes, although some leagues stipulate ten minutes for the course. It is shot at the PL 12 target.

2 The Elements of Pistol Shooting

SAFETY AND SECURITY

Accidents do not 'just happen' – they are caused – and to keep our sport safe it is necessary that everyone taking part in it acts safely at all times. Because pistols have short barrels and fit conveniently into the hand, it is all too easy to point them in any direction. For instance, if you are distracted when firing, you might turn around, still with your pistol in your hand, and without proper training you might well point the pistol away from the targets and at someone on the range. Therefore you must know how to be safe and what to do in certain situations. Safety must become a habit, and the safety rules must be learned and revised until they are second nature.

Safety in the Clubhouse

1. Always prove a pistol when removing it from its carrying case (*see* page 21).
2. Always prove a pistol when handing it to someone.
3. Always carry a pistol with the breech open.
4. If at all possible, keep pistols and ammunition separate.
5. Never handle a pistol without the owner's permission.
6. Never test the trigger without specific permission.
7. When 'firing' an unloaded pistol, point it in a safe direction, and never at anyone.
8. Never load a pistol or a magazine except on the range (loading a magazine is half-way to loading a pistol!).
9. *Never* point a pistol at anyone.

Safety on the Range

1. Prove your pistol when removing it from its case.
2. Know how the pistol you are going to shoot operates.
3. Do not handle pistols while people are forward of the firing line.
4. Do not load until told to do so by the range officer.
5. When a pistol is loaded, keep it pointing down range.
6. Keep your finger off the trigger until you are ready to shoot.
7. If you have to leave the firing point, or if there is some disturbance, unload your pistol and leave it with the breech open and muzzle pointing down range.
8. If there is any interruption after the command to load, unload and put your pistol on the bench with its muzzle pointing down range and the breech open. Then stand well back from the firing line, so that everyone can see that the pistol is safe.
9. After firing, prove the pistol, and ensure all magazines are empty.
10. Always prove your pistol before packing it away.

Safety in Transit

1. Keep your pistols out of sight when travelling in public.
2. Keep pistol and ammunition separate.
3. If you have to leave your car, take your pistol with you. If this is impossible, try to take some vital part with you (such as the breech block).

4. If you have to leave your pistols in a car, lock them into a steel box which is welded or securely bolted into the car's luggage boot. This box could be made to contain your ammunition as well, ideally in a separate compartment.

Safety in the Home

1. Always keep pistols and ammunition locked in a strong box or safe, preferably out of sight.
2. If possible, keep ammunition separate from pistols.
3. Keep children away from your pistols and ammunition, but train them in firearm safety, and let them handle your pistol under your supervision to satisfy their natural curiosity.
4. In storing your ammunition, consider the possibility of fire destroying that part of your home and use a fireproof container.

Proving a Pistol

Proving a pistol means ensuring that it is unloaded, not only to your own satisfaction, but also to the satisfaction of the range officer and other people around you.

To prove a single-shot pistol it is only necessary to open the breech and look inside to see that it is empty. To prove a revolver, open the cylinder, either by swinging it out of the frame or by 'breaking' it, and see that each chamber is empty. In some revolvers the cylinder does not come out of the frame, but there is a 'gate' at the rear and on one side of the cylinder. These revolvers need special care, as you have to open the gate and then inspect each chamber one by one as you turn the cylinder around.

To prove a semi-automatic pistol, first remove the magazine, then draw back the slide (the breech block) and lock it to the rear. In some makes of semi-automatic you must draw the slide back before you can remove the magazine. Look in the breech and ensure that it is empty; then look to see that a cartridge has not been held on the face of the breech block due to a faulty ejector. If the slide does not lock in

the rear position, insert a wooden or plastic wedge to hold the action open.

BASIC TECHNIQUE

The basic principles of pistol shooting are so important it is impossible to over-emphasise how fully they must be understood and applied. We therefore recommend that you return to this section and reread it from time to time. There is no magic about pistol shooting – success will go to those who fully understand the basic principles and apply them all the time. Certain UIT disciplines call for some modification of the basic technique, but they do not replace it. The basic principles are the foundation upon which other techniques may be built.

The advice which follows is not dogmatic; rather, it consists of recommendations to which there will always be exceptions. There are different ways of doing certain things and, depending upon your physique and mentality, you may find one more effective than another. Try the method suggested here first and if, after you have diligently practised it, you find another more successful, then by all means use that other method.

STANCE

To shoot successfully it is necessary to maintain a stable firing position which will allow the pistol to be held at arm's length with as little movement as possible. To do this you need to use every muscle in your body: from the toes up through your ankles, legs and thighs to the trunk and on to the arm, wrist and fingers, neck and even the eye muscles. All these must be controlled but not strained.

There are various stances which can be used to meet different situations, and these will also vary with individual physique, but the fundamental consideration is to adopt a stance which will help to keep your body, and hence your pistol, as still as possible.

If you stand with your feet together, your

In-line stance

Oblique stance

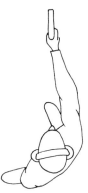

Square or open stance

Notice that the eye is nearer the sights in the square stance.

body will sway in any direction and, indeed, can possibly gyrate, so you must move your feet apart. Now with feet apart, if you stand square to the target you will have a tendency to sway forwards and backwards, giving rise to a vertically displaced group of shots on the target. Conversely, if you stand with your shoulders pointing in line to the target you will still sway forwards and backwards but now the shots will be spread horizontally across the target.

It is obvious that these are unstable positions; you need to adopt a position which will reduce body sway to a minimum. This can be achieved by adopting what is called the 'oblique' stance. Your feet should be placed at least as far apart as your shoulders (wider if you are shooting in a strong wind), with your body facing 45 degrees away from the target, and your feet making an angle of 60 to 70 degrees between them. Your weight should be evenly balanced between each foot, and each foot should be taking your weight evenly over the whole bottom of the foot and toes. If you feel there is more pressure on the inside of your feet, then they are probably too far apart.

Your body should be upright, with your head held up. There is a tendency to hunch your shooting shoulder and to lower your head into

your extended arm. Do not do this. Look through the centre of your eye, not out of a corner or edge. Not only will this avoid the effects of astigmatism, it will also help you to keep your head in a consistent position. The arm holding the pistol should be straight, not bent at the elbow. The non-shooting arm must

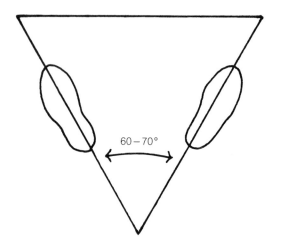

A stable position is created when the body's centre of gravity, with pistol raised on aim, falls within the triangle set out by the feet being approximately 60 to 70 degrees to each other and a shoulder width apart at the heels.

be anchored to prevent it from moving about, movement which can be transmitted through your shoulders to your shooting arm. Place your non-shooting hand in a trouser or jacket pocket, or put your thumb in a waistband or belt. Do anything which is effective and comfortable but make sure that you do not raise or lower your non-shooting shoulder. Your shoulders should be level. Also ensure that you do not bring your non-shooting arm too far across the front of the body as this will tend to compress your rib-cage and thus restrict your lung capacity. If you have no other option, you may place your non-shooting hand on your hip.

Each time you set yourself up to shoot, it is necessary to find your correct stance. This is done in the following way:

1. Stand in approximately the right position, facing 45 degrees away from the target, with your unloaded pistol correctly held.

2. Close your eyes.
3. Raise your pistol and, keeping your eyes closed, wiggle your body and arm about. It will settle into its natural and comfortable position.
4. Open your eyes and see where the sights are pointing. If they are not pointing at the centre of the target, or at a vertical line passing through its centre, move your feet to align the sights with the centre of the target, keeping the angle between your body and your arm constant. If you need to turn to your right (and are right-handed) then move your left foot forward and pivot on your right foot. A left-handed shooter will move the right foot back and pivot on the left foot.
5. Now repeat the procedure to ensure you have found your correct position. Carry out this procedure every time you move your feet during shooting.

You may see some shooters mark around their

Square or an open stance – the eye is nearer to the sights, making focus difficult.

Oblique stance – the most stable position.

In-line stance – this position gives the greatest possible distance between eye and sights.

Incorrect oblique stance – the head is lowered into the shoulder so that the shooter looks through the edge of his eye causing distortion of vision.

feet with chalk, so that they can place their feet in the same position each time without carrying out the procedure just described. However, this is wrong. Your stance will alter during your shoot due to such factors as tiredness, heat or cold, changing wind and muscular exercise. Therefore find the correct stance each time you pick up your pistol if you have moved your feet.

One advantage gained by using the oblique stance is that your body's centre of gravity will be within a triangle subtended by your feet. If your body is kept erect within this triangle you will preserve your balance with the least expenditure of effort, avoiding strain, and will therefore be capable of concentrating the rest of your resources on the other factors controlling the release of a good shot.

For the UIT disciplines certain modifications to the oblique stance will be required to meet specific circumstances. These do not detract from the basic principle that you need to adopt a good stance which will keep your shooting arm steady with the minimum of muscular effort. It is essential that you provide a steady platform from which to launch consistently good shots.

Do remember when thinking about your stance that you should avoid tension in any of your muscles. Where possible they should be controlled but relaxed. Tense muscles soon tire, causing you to lose control over them. In particular relax your jaw, stomach and bottom – these are places where stress can be noticed.

Dr D.R. Young (USA) shooting to win the UIT Standard Pistol Championship with a very creditable score of 577 points, at the 1985 British Pistol Championships at Bisley. Note his very positive stance, with feet well apart.

Shooting the rapid-fire event.

BREATHING

Breathing is closely related to stance as it concerns the body's position and its effect upon the movement of the pistol. As you breathe, your rib-cage expands and contracts, thus causing movement to your extended arm. It is therefore necessary to stop this movement whilst you are taking aim and releasing your shot by stopping breathing during these processes. This is unfortunate as we need as much freshly oxygenated blood as we can get to maintain the body at optimum performance when pistol shooting. So, before coming on aim

and starting to hold your breath, you should fill your lungs with fresh air. Do not overdo this or you may suffer the effects of hyper-ventilation, such as increased pulse-rate and dizziness.

In everyday activities we only use the top part of our lungs with the result that carbon dioxide and other gases accumulate in the bottom. Like other athletes, you will have got rid of these waste products from your lungs when you were doing your daily physical training and you will have accustomed your lungs to full inflation, so that they are able to absorb the total amount of oxygen available to them. Smoking tobacco is not recommended as this severely limits the ability of the lungs to pass oxygen to the blood stream.

Take a succession of deep breaths and fully expel them, trying to breathe with your

25

diaphragm so that you use the bottom as well as the upper part of the lungs. This activity will cause your heart to beat more quickly to take advantage of the oxygen available to the blood. At this point you must wait for a while, breathing lightly, while your pulse-rate slows down. The fitter you are, the quicker your pulse returns to normality, and indeed, the less effect deep breathing has upon it.

Personal experiment will show you that it is uncomfortable to hold your breath with the lungs either full or empty; an intermediate position is preferable, with the lungs half empty. Having taken several deep breaths and allowed your pulse-rate time to decline, take a final deep breath as you raise your pistol and then gently breathe out about half of it as the pistol settles into the aiming position. Once the shot has been fired, take a few more deep breaths and repeat the cycle for each successive shot.

Physical training will improve your breathing, lung capacity and the amount of oxygen in your blood. Aerobic exercises such as swimming, skipping, fast walking, and running are particularly useful for this.

The importance of correct breathing cannot be over-emphasised. Success in pistol shooting requires great concentration and keenly focused eyesight, and for these to be achieved the blood which fuels the body's processes must be fully oxygenated. Oxygenated blood is needed for the brain to function efficiently, for the eye to see and to focus correctly and for the muscles throughout the body to work without undue fatigue. More than this, by adopting a certain breathing rhythm, the brain can measure the elapse of time (*see* page 88).

GRIP

Your hold on a pistol's butt is called 'grip', and hence the butt of a pistol is often called the grip, or, as they are usually made in two halves, the grips. You do not hold a pistol as you would a tennis racket, for example, by wrapping your fingers all around the handle.

Taking Hold

Pick up the pistol with your non-shooting hand, holding it by its barrel, and feed the butt into your shooting hand. Your shooting hand should have the thumb and fingers wide apart. Press the pistol firmly into the palm of the hand, and then close your second and third fingers on to the butt, keeping the first finger (the trigger finger) clear. Hold the butt as high up as possible so that when the pistol fires, the fulcrum about which the pistol will rotate on the recoil is as high as possible to reduce the upward movement of the muzzle. Hold the pistol so that the barrel is in line with your forearm so that the recoil is absorbed along the arm, straight into the shoulder and hence the body. Ideally the pistol should form a natural extension of your arm.

The trigger finger should not touch the frame of the pistol so that movement is not transmitted

Taking the grip *(a)* *The pistol is being offered to the shooting hand which is open to receive it.*

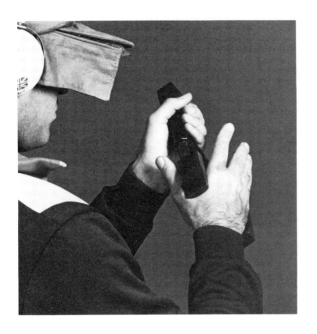

Taking the grip *(b)* *The butt is pushed firmly into the palm with the hand as high up as possible. The barrel forms an extension of the forearm in both vertical and horizontal planes.*

Taking the grip *(c)* *The second and third fingers are folded on the front of the butt and push the butt back into the palm. The thumb is kept clear.*

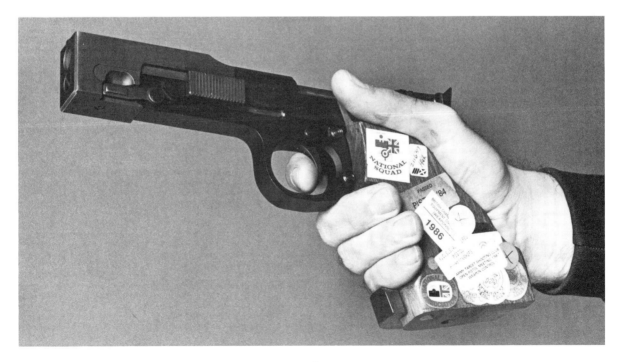

Taking the grip *(d)* *The thumb is relaxed and the trigger finger correctly located on the bottom of the trigger to obtain the best leverage.*

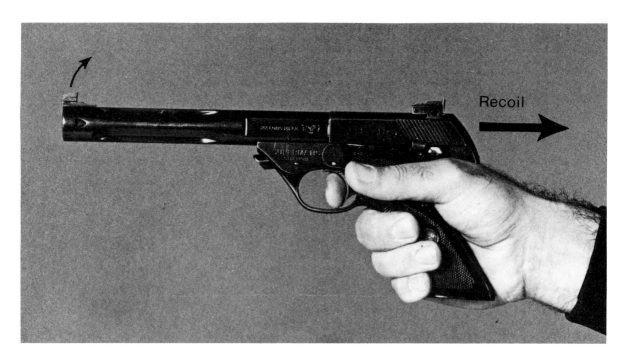

Recoil

Right   *The pistol is held as high up the butt as possible, thus reducing the tendency for the muzzle to rise, and allowing the recoil to be absorbed through the arm.*

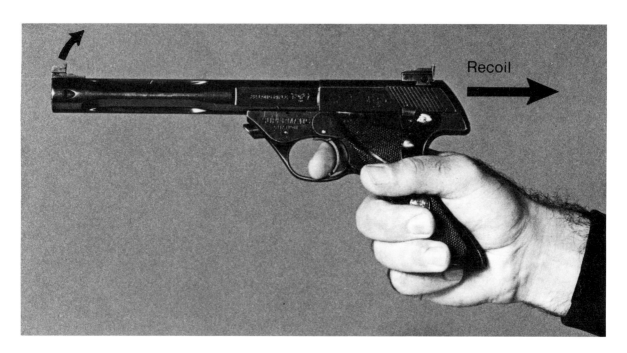

Recoil

Wrong   *Holding the pistol too low, thus lowering the centre of balance and causing greater upward movement of the muzzle when the pistol recoils.*

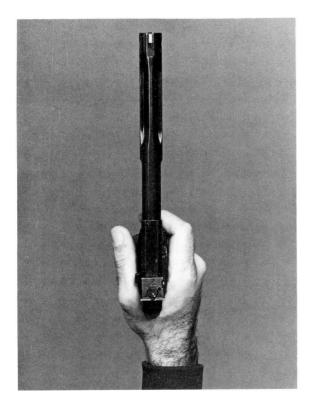

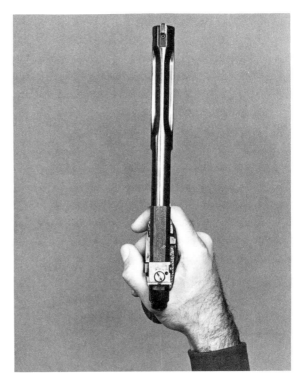

Right   *The barrel forms an extension of the forearm so that recoil is absorbed straight along the arm and into the body.*

Wrong   *The hand is too far round the butt so that the pistol turns about the centre of balance on recoil, deflecting the muzzle sideways.*

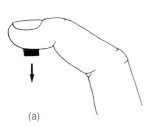

(a)

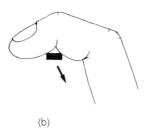

(b)

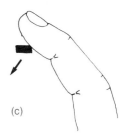

(c)

(a) Right   *The finger is squeezing straight to the rear with the centre of the first pad.*
(b) Wrong   *The finger is too far over the trigger, pulling the trigger towards the hand.*
(c) Wrong   *Too little of the finger is on the trigger, pushing the trigger to one side.*

to the pistol as your finger moves to the rear when squeezing the trigger. The centre of the first pad of your index finger should press the trigger straight to the rear along the fore and aft axis of the barrel. There should be no sideways pressure on the trigger. If just the tip of your finger is touching the trigger it may slip off, or it may press the trigger sideways. Alternatively, if too much of your finger is projecting across the trigger it will pull the trigger sideways towards your hand. In either extreme position it will make the trigger weight feel heavier than it actually is, partly because you are not obtaining the best leverage and partly because you will be trying to press the trigger sideways against the side of the frame.

The little finger should exert very little pressure on the butt because it may tend to pull the muzzle down as the pistol fires. The thumb should not exert any pressure on the grip, but should be relaxed so that the muscles at its base exert a consistent pressure at the palm of the hand. Try to imagine that your thumb has been cut off at its first joint! Either let it lie relaxed along the grip, or keep it clear of the grip altogether – but not strained.

You will see from this that it is the middle and the third finger which really control the grip and they exert a constant pressure on the fore and aft surfaces of the grips. This is important – the pressure must be kept in the fore and aft line.

These two fingers squeeze the butt into the palm of the hand.

Uniformity

In order to place all your shots in as small a group as possible, the pistol must be gripped with the same pressure and applied to the same parts of the butt for each shot. Consistency is of the utmost importance. Therefore practise at home, picking up your pistol and gripping it until it becomes second nature.

Pressure

The pistol must be held tight enough to prevent it moving in the hand when the shot fires. That is to say, the pressure must control the recoil. The recoil will vary from nil with a recoil-less air pistol to quite a considerable pressure with a centre-fire pistol shooting a magnum cartridge. You must therefore hold the centre-fire pistol tighter than you need hold the air pistol. The .22 rim-fire pistol will be in between. You will need to tighten your grip when firing several shots in rapid succession, to control the repeated recoil effect. But the amount of pressure applied must be consistent for the particular discipline, or series of shots, you are firing.

If you apply too much pressure you will reach

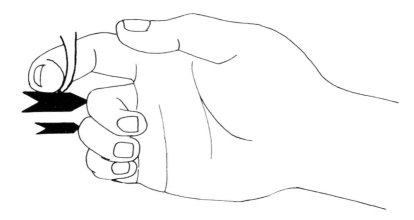

The relative strength and direction of the grip pressure: the thumb and little finger exert no pressure.

a point where your muscles tremble uncontrollably. If this occurs, put the pistol down, pause for a moment, and then take a fresh hold using less pressure. It is very difficult merely to relax the pressure you have applied; and it is almost inevitable that your grip would be incorrect.

Due to the construction of the muscles, tendons and nerves in your hand and their interrelationship, the tighter your middle and third fingers grip, the more difficult it becomes to apply very gentle pressure with your index finger. The pressure you apply in holding the grip should be proportional to the trigger pressure. For instance, if you are shooting an air pistol with only 500g trigger weight, you do not want to hold the grip more tightly than is necessary to keep the pistol firmly in your hand during the let-off procedure.

Effect of Temperature

If the weather is warm or if you are shooting in a warm range, it is likely that your hand will swell as the blood flow to it is stimulated in an attempt to dissipate the heat in your hand. Conversely, in cold weather your hand will contract. In either circumstance you will be compelled to take a different grip from that which you would otherwise use. It is useful to have a towel with you to dry a sweaty hand, and talc can help to maintain your grip in adverse conditions. When conditions are cold, a pocket hand-warmer will help you to feel the trigger more precisely and give comfort to your other fingers. If you use an anatomical grip (one shaped to your own hand) you may need to make adjustments to its fit in very warm or very cold weather, by altering the position of the palm shelf.

Grips

As a beginner, you should use the factory-made grips with which your pistol is fitted when new. But as you progress and gain experience, you will almost certainly find that you need grips shaped to your own hand, known as anatomical grips. You can file or carve pieces away or add

plastic wood to make up deficiencies. Your aim should be to have a grip which is comfortable, which keeps as much of the surface of your hand in contact with it as possible, which ensures that the pistol will 'point' whenever it is brought on aim, and which conforms with the rules laid down for the particular discipline. By 'pointing' it is meant that as the arm is raised into the aiming position, the foresight will automatically be in the centre of the rearsight, without you having to bend your wrist. Instead of altering your grips you may decide to have a pair made for you by one of the several specialist grip makers.

TRIGGER CONTROL

Correct trigger control is probably the most important factor in firing an accurate shot. All the effort and concentration you have put into obtaining the correct stance, breath control and aiming can be wasted by faulty trigger control.

Correct trigger control may be considered in three stages:

1. *Where* to apply the pressure to the trigger.
2. *When* to apply the pressure to the trigger.
3. *How* to apply the pressure to the trigger.

Where

The index finger (first finger) must apply pressure to the trigger directly to the rear, in line with the fore and aft axis of the barrel. Any variation from this direct line will cause angular errors due to sight disturbance, and may also induce a snatched shot, due to the trigger weight feeling too heavy if you are pressing it to the side. The part of the finger touching the trigger must move in a straight line, in the fore and aft axis, and be at right angles to the trigger at the moment of let-off.

The index finger must be correctly placed on the trigger and in exactly the same position for every shot. The centre of the first pad of the index finger should touch the trigger fairly near the tip of the trigger. In this position it can obtain the best leverage, thus reducing the

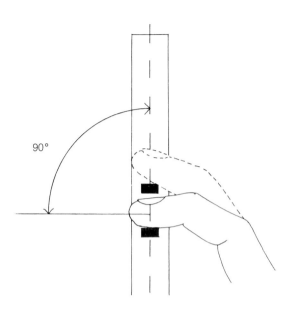

The trigger finger should be at 90 degrees to the fore and aft line of the barrel at the moment of trigger release.

Testing the trigger pull. Here a 500g weight is being used to test an air pistol. Note that the barrel must be vertical while the weight is lifted clear of the table.

amount of pressure you will have to apply to overcome the weight of the trigger mechanism. In competition, triggers are set to lift a certain weight before they will release. For UIT standard pistol this weight is 1kg, for an air pistol it is 500g, and for American conventional small-bore shooting it is 2lb.

If the finger is put too far over the trigger, the finger will not exert the optimum pressure and it is inevitable that it will press the trigger from the far side (that is, pull the trigger towards your hand), causing the muzzle to move in the opposite direction as the pistol recoils on firing. Conversely, if only the tip of the finger touches the trigger, you will again not exert the best pressure and you may feel your finger is slipping off the trigger; but you will also push the trigger sideways (away from your hand), deflecting the muzzle at shot release.

If the finger touches the trigger well up towards the barrel it loses the advantage of leverage, and the trigger will not only feel heavier than it really is, it will feel slightly different for each shot because you will not be

able to be consistent in the positioning of your finger.

Apart from the centre of the first pad touching the trigger, the rest of the finger should not touch the frame or butt to avoid disturbing the pistol as the finger moves backwards. As the shot breaks, there are rapid muscular movements in the lower part of the index finger which will disturb the pistol if they touch the grip.

Your fingertip moves in an arc resulting from the effect of the two hinges provided by the first and second finger joints, and it cannot therefore be at right angles to the trigger during the whole of the let-off process. The finger needs to be at right angles to the trigger at the moment of let-

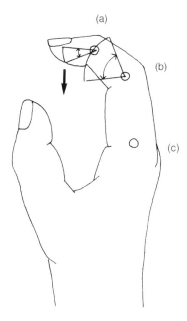

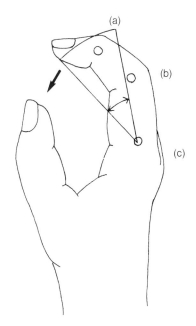

Right *Pressure is applied to the trigger by movement at joints (a) and (b), pressing the trigger straight to the rear in line with the barrel.*

Wrong *Movement at joint (c) causes a sideways pressure on the trigger.*

The Britarm 2000 Mk II, showing its anatomical trigger and the shaft along which it can be moved in the fore and aft axis to suit your grip and finger size.

33

Adjusting the position of the trigger on a Feinwerkbau CO₂ pistol.

off. Some adjustment may be necessary to achieve this comfortably. In certain pistols this can be done by moving the position of the trigger in its fore and aft travel, in others you may need to alter the shape of the butt to adjust the position of your finger relative to the trigger.

When

The trigger release should be timed to coincide with the optimum point of the other factors affecting the shot release. In slow-fire shooting this will be from five to ten seconds after taking up the aim. Obviously in rapid-fire shooting you must build up the pressure on the trigger much more quickly to suit the time available in the particular discipline being shot. Good

trigger control has to be mastered in slow-fire shooting before you progress to rapid-fire techniques. In a way, rapid-fire shooting is only slow-fire shooting done quickly, at least as far as trigger control is concerned.

How

Trigger systems vary and the two most likely to be met are those in which there is a definite first and second pressure (this is the more common type) or those where the trigger has a roll-over mechanism. In the latter type there is no stop in the application of pressure, and it must be applied in one smooth, continuous action. With the other types which have two stages of pressure, the first should be taken up and held early in the aiming process, and then the extra

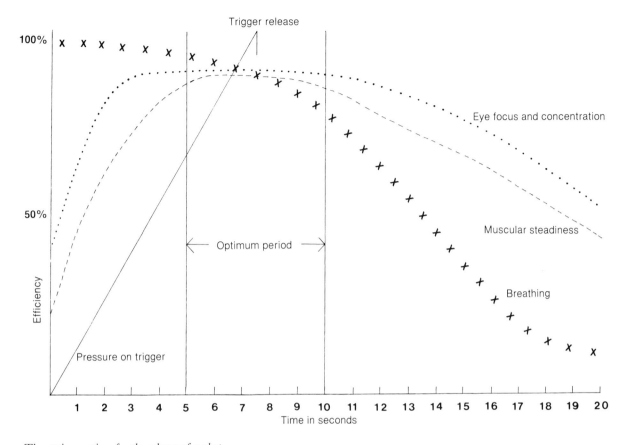

The optimum time for the release of a shot.

pressure should be applied smoothly until the trigger is released.

At no time should the trigger be pulled or snatched. The pressure on the trigger must be a squeeze. While you are in the aiming position, and the correct sight picture is being maintained, the message from your brain to your trigger finger is: '... going ... going ... going ... (bang) – hold steady ... steady ... steady'. Never does the brain send the message 'fire'. If it did, a snatch would surely result. All the time the eye is telling the brain that the sight picture is correct, and the aim is acceptable, the brain will be telling the finger to squeeze. In a way, when the shot breaks you should be surprised, yet remain in full control.

If the sight picture is not exactly right, or if the aim passes out of tolerance, or if any other factor feels wrong then *immediately* take your

finger off the trigger. Do not hesitate, as the shot may be just about to break and a fraction more pressure on the trigger will cause it to do so. Practise the habit of slamming your finger forward and off the trigger if all is not right. Then come down off aim and relax, regain your concentration and prepare to fire again. Too often even expert shooters have lost valuable points through being slow to take their finger off the trigger when conditions were not correct.

When you are learning to shoot a pistol there is a temptation to try to fire the shot every time you bring a loaded pistol into the aiming position. Once you have overcome this temptation, and learned the value of not releasing a shot when everything is not exactly right, you will be well on the way to becoming a good shooter.

Always remember that a good score is made

35

not so much by firing perfect shots, but by eliminating the bad shots. Very few people can pick up a pistol confident that their shot will definitely be in the X-ring – nor would anyone be advised to try that approach. What you should try to do is to launch each shot perfectly, which is not quite the same thing. Stop whenever something is not right and try again when matters have been corrected; it is too late to do anything about it once the trigger has released.

Improving Trigger Control

You can improve your trigger control with various exercises:

1.   Practise positioning your finger on the trigger so that it becomes second nature each time you take your grip on the pistol. With sufficient practice you will immediately know when your finger is not in the correct position. You can, and should, practise this at home. Constant practice will enable you to memorise how the trigger should feel, and therefore to recognise when the right part of your finger is touching the correct place on the trigger. When you have been practising this for some time, try doing it with your eyes closed. This will help you to visualise where your finger is on the trigger. Eventually you will memorise this feel to the extent that you can actually practise visualising your finger on the trigger even when you do not have a pistol in your hand.

2.   Practise 'dry firing' to co-ordinate your brain and muscles. Here again, you can and should practise at home. Place a small aiming mark, or a white circle on a black background, on a wall and aim your *unloaded* pistol at it. Some pistols have a special facility to enable you to dry fire them without harm to the firing pin, but for the others you will need to insert an empty case in the breech to absorb the blow from the firing pin, or you can buy special dummy cartridges for this purpose. What you want to avoid is letting the firing pin strike the face of the breech, or even come against the edge of the firing pin hole. If this happens once in a while, no harm will be done, but if it is

repeated, you can damage both the firing pin and the part it strikes.

3.   On the range you can practise good trigger control by shooting at a blank card. Turn the target round and shoot at its back. With no aiming mark to distract you, you can concentrate on the sight picture and the trigger release. Without an aiming mark, and with your hand and pistol hiding the bottom of the target, you will have no means of assessing the vertical position of the sights and will therefore shoot a vertically elongated group. The eye can determine the horizontal middle of the card quite easily as far as this exercise is concerned. You may be surprised at first at the small-sized groups your shots make. If shots appear outside the vertical group to the sides you can be sure that you pushed or pulled the trigger (given that you maintained a reasonable sight picture).

This exercise is not only for beginners; every shooter should practise it from time to time to sharpen his performance. If you are to succeed as a pistol shooter, *the basic techniques must always be applied*.

Faults

1.   *Snatching*: too rapid a build-up of pressure on the trigger causes it to continue to move to the rear after the sear has released the firing mechanism, with the result that the pistol is jerked off aim while the bullet is travelling up the barrel. A snatch can also be caused by premeditating the shot – where the brain has ordered the trigger finger to *fire*, instead of saying 'squeeze … squeeze …', to build up the pressure smoothly and steadily.

Snatching is shown by an excessive movement of the pistol at the moment of trigger release. Shots often go low left or low right in these circumstances. This may be due to flinching at the thought of the coming explosion and recoil, showing that you are not using the correct mental technique: once again you are sending the message 'fire' to your finger, thus jerking the pistol while the bullet is still travelling up the barrel.

One remedy, apart from the dry training

exercise described above, is for your coach to load your pistol for you. Occasionally he will insert a dummy round along with the live ones. You will not know when such a round has been fed into the breech, and when the trigger releases, the pistol should not move at all. It is quite illuminating to see how much 'recoil' can occur with such a 'misfire'. All the movement resulting from this exercise comes from bad trigger control, and once you recognise this you should be well on the way to correcting it.

2. *Pushing*: if a right-handed shooter pushes the shot, by not having his finger far enough across the trigger, the shot will go to the left. The remedy is to ensure that the finger is properly positioned on the correct part of the trigger.

3. *Pulling*: if a right-handed shooter pulls the shot, by having too much of the finger across the trigger, the shot will go to the right. The remedy, once again, is to ensure that the finger is correctly placed on the trigger and to carry out plenty of dry training so that the correct position is learned.

4. *Holding on aim too long*: this is the opposite of snatching. If the pressure is applied too slowly, the shot will not be released while all the factors contributing to an accurate release are at their optimum. Errors due to poor muscular action resulting from lack of oxygen in the blood, loss of concentration, loss of clear focus and muscular tremor will lead to an inaccurate release. Such shots will have a random error.

This is a common mistake, but one which can be overcome by dry training. Training will co-ordinate the brain and muscles in applying positive pressure build-up on the trigger in a time-scale dictated by the discipline being practised.

Sometimes holding on aim too long arises because the shooter lacks confidence and is afraid of firing a bad shot. This can be overcome by firing shots in pairs. Once the first shot has been fired, do not bring the gun down but recover the aiming position and immediately release a second aimed shot. Of course, this is not possible if you are using a single shot pistol.

FOLLOW-THROUGH

As in other sports, the follow-through is an important part of completing the action. Firing a shot does not end with the release of the firing pin or hammer – it ends when the bullet has gone through the target, and when you have recovered from the firing process. When the shot breaks, you should stay on aim for a few seconds. Take a mental photograph of where your sights were the moment the trigger released, and also note where they have settled during your follow-through. Your image of the sight picture at the moment the shot broke will enable you to say where your shot has hit the target. This is known as 'calling the shot'. After the follow-through has been completed, you may look through your telescope to confirm your shot's position. If you are to become proficient in pistol shooting, you will need to be able to call your shots with a fair degree of accuracy. But do not worry if at first you are unable to do this, as it is a skill which will develop with experience if you keep trying to do it.

There is more to the follow-through than calling the shot. If your brain sends the message to your trigger finger of 'squeeze . . . squeeze . . .', and not the message 'fire', you should not be capable of immediate reaction when the shot breaks. All your mental and physical functions should continue to concentrate on maintaining the correct sight picture and on keeping the pistol as still as possible. The knowledge that after the shot has gone you are going to remain still during the follow-through helps you to keep steady at the moment of shot release. You know that whatever happens you are going to keep your pistol as still as possible and you are going to concentrate your attention on the aiming and let-off processes, so there is no tendency to relax prematurely, that is, before the shot has left the barrel. This could well happen if you have not developed the follow-through technique. Thus, a good follow-through helps you to maintain a steady and stable position right through the let-off.

Conversely, without a good follow-through,

your concentration will reduce dramatically and your muscles will relax as soon as your shot is released. This means you could easily flick the bullet whilst it is still in the barrel – this is especially likely with an air pistol where the pellet travels comparatively slowly.

If you do not make a conscious effort to develop your follow-through, there is a good chance that you will gradually end your aiming and let-off procedures fractionally earlier, in other words, you will anticipate the shot's release. Inevitably this will result in a snatch and loss of concentration at the vital moment when all your faculties should have been at their greatest efficiency – that moment just before shot release. Of course, you will not know when that moment is going to occur, and that is why a good follow-through is so important.

SIGHT PICTURE AND AIMING

Aim is the correct positioning of the sights in relation to the target, whilst sight picture is the positioning of the foresight in relation to the rearsight.

With the pistol held at arm's length the first object your eye will see is the rearsight; next will be the foresight and then, much further away, will be the target, with its aiming mark. Now, your eye cannot focus on three objects at different distances at the same time. You may think you can see all three at once; but what your eye is actually doing is focusing on one, then on another, and changing its focal length very quickly from one object to the next and back again. When you are young this appears to be acceptable; but as you age, your eyes become less accommodating. It is therefore as well to start as you intend to go on.

Of the three objects to be seen – the rearsight, the foresight and the target – it is the foresight which is the most important, as this shows where the barrel is pointing; then comes the rearsight, and last of all in importance comes the target itself. This may seem strange, and beginners usually think that they should focus on the target. However, any error in aligning the foresight in the rearsight will cause an angular error, which will increase in its effect the further the bullet travels as it forms an angle between the line of the barrel (the line of fire) and the line of sight. This error can be in the vertical plane or the horizontal plane, or in a combination of the two. Angular errors must be eliminated completely.

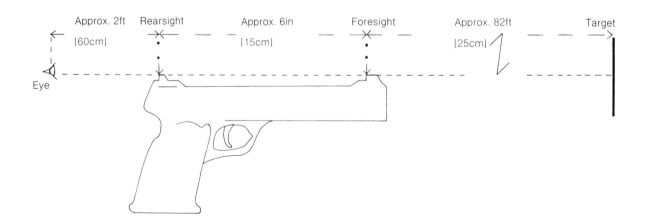

The eye cannot focus simultaneously on three objects at different distances.

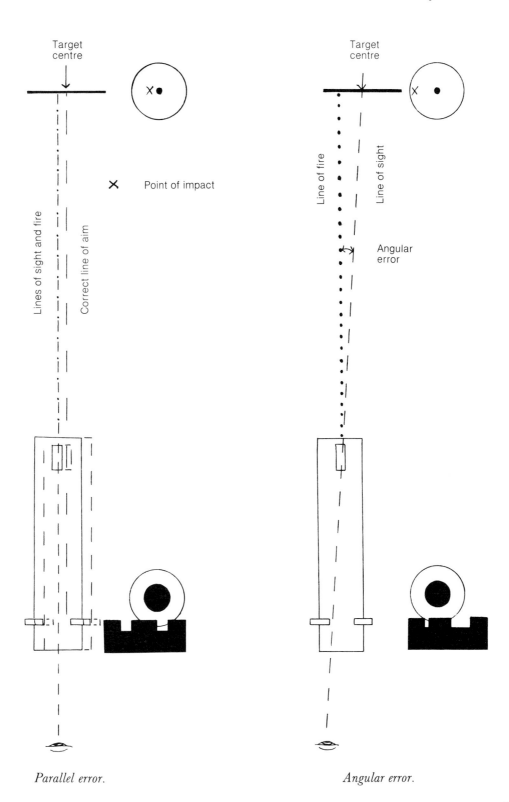

Parallel error.   *Angular error.*

For this reason, you must be able to see your sights, especially the foresight, clearly. It is therefore on the foresight that you must focus your eye. To enable you to do this, you may need to visit an optician and have a pair of shooting glasses made. Do impress upon your optician that you need to see the foresight clearly, in other words an object some six inches (15 centimetres) beyond your hand outstretched at arm's length. It is a good idea to take your pistol with you, but do make sure that the optician and his staff know that it is unloaded and safe. At the same time as you have a lens made which will permit you to focus clearly on the foresight, you should have a plain, toughened glass put in the other eyepiece as a precaution, to prevent spent gases or fragments entering your eye – especially if you are going to shoot centre fire.

So, the vital part of the aiming process is a clear sight picture and this can only be achieved when your eye is focused on the foresight. It will then see the foresight clearly, the rearsight will not be quite so clear and the target will appear slightly blurred. It is worth remembering that in target pistol shooting the target will always be in the same position – it is not going to move (apart from turning on its vertical axis), so it does not matter if it does appear slightly blurred.

When sighting, many people close the eye they are not using. This is acceptable, but it is better not to close it because if you do, you tend to close your sighting eye a little in sympathy. A better answer to the problem is to blank off the non-sighting eye with a screen which can be fitted to your shooting glasses. This screen should be hinged at the top so that you can move it out of the way when you wish to use your telescope. The screen can be opaque, but it is better to have one which is translucent, provided you cannot see objects through it. A translucent screen will let light enter the eye which will help your total vision, as your two eyes tend to work in unison.

It is as well to know which is your master eye, as, if you are right-handed and have poor vision in your right eye but good vision in your left

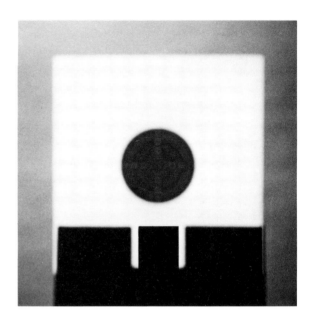

A correct sight picture, with sharp foresight, clear rearsight and target blurred.

eye, something needs to be done to help you overcome this handicap. Most people have a dominant eye; in some people the dominance moves from one eye to the other, perhaps in relation to fatigue. Anyway, to find which is your master eye at any time, make a circle with the index finger and thumb of one hand and hold this out at arm's length in front of you. Now sight some object about ten feet (three metres) away, such as a light switch across the room. Now close one eye and see if the object is still encircled. Then open that eye and close the other one. You will see that only one eye aligns the circle with the object, and that eye is your master eye.

If your master eye is on the opposite side of your body from the hand you normally use, and you have trouble focusing well with your weak eye, you should consider learning to shoot with your other hand. Pistol grips are made for either left or right-handed users.

To help you increase your depth of focus it is permitted to use an orthoptic. This is a device which is fitted to your shooting glasses, and which has an adjustable iris. When you look through this it acts rather like a pin-hole camera. Whilst a small opening will provide the greatest focal depth, it will also reduce the amount of light which passes through the hole. The way an orthoptic should be used is to have as large an opening as possible compatible with seeing your foresight sharply and your rearsight reasonably clearly. Make sure that the orthoptic is at right angles to your line of sight in both the vertical and horizontal planes. If it is not, you will not be looking through a round hole but an elongated one, and it will not be used to best advantage.

Sight Picture

The correct sight picture occurs when the top of the foresight is exactly level with the top of the rearsight, and the gap either side of the fore-sight blade in the rearsight notch is the same. *There is no room for error.* Any error in this alignment will produce an angular error.

To help you focus on the foresight and to see the whole sight picture as sharply as possible, the sights should be blackened. The best results are achieved by blacking the back and the top of the sights with carbide soot. This gives a very intense, even, matt black. Special lamps burning calcium carbide are available for this purpose, or a miner's lamp can be used. Camphor will give quite good results, as will a candle flame, and even a match's soot is better than nothing as a last resort. There is a sight-

Blackening the sights with soot from a carbide flame.

blacking liquid on the market which you paint on, but it does not give as even or as intense a black as carbide soot. Whatever you use, always blacken your sights before shooting. Since soot is easily rubbed off, it is necessary to blacken your sights before each match. Do not leave this to the last minute before shooting, as the bright light from the carbide flame will unsettle your vision for a considerable period afterwards. While it is difficult not to look at the flame when you are blacking your sights, you should avoid staring at it. It can help if you close your sighting eye while you do this job.

Whilst the use of blackened sights is advisable for all disciplines of pistol shooting, you may be tempted to try using coloured sights at times to help you see your sights either more clearly or more quickly. Various combinations of colours have been tried: white fore and rearsights, white foresight with black rearsight, orange sights, yellow sights, fluorescent colours, and various permutations of these. However, most shooters return to using the matt black sights in

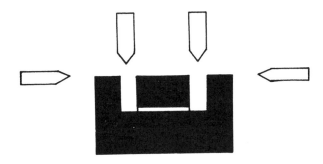

A correct sight picture: the foresight is level with the shoulders of the rearsight, with equal gaps either side of the foresight.

the end, even for shooting on the black rapid-fire target.

To help you obtain the correct sight picture every time you take aim, you should memorise what the correct sight picture looks like. You can do this by carefully drawing the theoretical picture on a piece of card. This should be drawn in matt black ink, a little larger than actual size. You should look at it frequently to memorise the picture, not just when you are shooting. Put it up in your home and look at it during your daily routine. When you are shooting, place it on the bench in front of you and look at it between shots. Not only will this help you to detect when your sights are not quite correctly aligned, it will also alter your focal length between aiming and so rest your eyes.

Aim

The correct aim is achieved when the correct sight picture is placed against an imaginary vertical line passing through the centre of the target. You do not usually aim at the target's centre but at a point somewhere below the aiming mark. There are two reasons for this:

1.   No one can hold a pistol absolutely still and so it will move about within a certain area of tolerance while you are on aim. If you try to aim at a precise aiming mark, this area of movement will be very apparent and will upset your concentration. It will also almost certainly make you hold your aim too long in an effort to release the shot when the wobble has decreased. The chances are that it will never get less and will only increase. You will hold on aim too long and, if you persist in trying to let the shot go, the result will be a wide error.

2.   The second reason why you should aim below the aiming mark is that here you will have an uninterrupted view of your sights. Without the aiming mark to distract you, you can concentrate on maintaining the correct sight picture. Your sights will show up clearly against the creamy-white target, instead of being lost against the black aiming mark. Remember, it is vital that you have the correct sight picture when the shot is released to avoid an angular error.

Aiming below the aiming mark in this way is known as 'area aiming' and, in this instance, it is a six o'clock area aim. In shooting, the clock-face is used to describe direction from the centre of the target. Imagine that a twelve-hour clock-face is superimposed on the target. A shot above the centre, on a vertical line passing through the

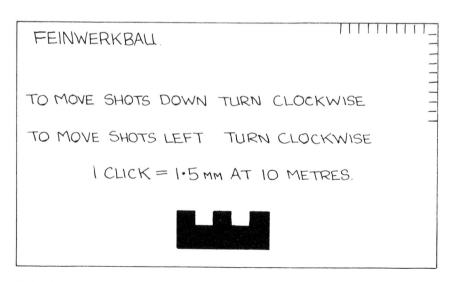

Sight alteration card with 'epsilon' memoriser.

Area aim at six o'clock; although you aim below the aiming mark, the sights are set to cause the bullet to hit the target's centre, leaving your sight picture undisturbed by the aiming mark itself.

A parallel error: a correct sight picture, but the aim is slightly displaced to the left.

middle, would be said to be at 12 o'clock. A shot off to the right, but level with the centre of the target, would be said to be at three o'clock, and so on. Distance from the centre is described by the scoring ring in which the shot has gone.

When taking a six o'clock area aim you should aim somewhere around a third to half the way between the bottom of the aiming mark and the bottom of the target. Just where you aim will depend upon your ability to judge the width of the white gap consistently, but you need to be sufficiently far from the black that it does not distract you. If you have a wide area of wobble, you may need to aim further below the black than if you have a small area of wobble.

The fact that you aim your pistol well below the centre of the target has no effect on where the bullets strike it, because you offset your sights to compensate for this point of aim. With most pistols you alter the height of the rearsight to allow for this displacement, although there are a few pistols where you alter the height of the foresight to make a similar adjustment.

If you are ever in doubt about which way to alter your sights, draw yourself a sketch showing the line of fire (that is, the line of the barrel), the line of sight, the point of impact of your shots, the centre of the target, and the new line of fire needed to make the point of impact coincide with the centre of the target.

If your eyesight is adaptable, such as when you are young, there can be an argument for taking what is called a tangential aim at six o'clock. That is, placing your sight picture so that the aiming mark just rests on top of the foresight. This can give you a very precise point of aim, but it is very tiring for the eye over any length of time, and you are fighting to hold your pistol very still. It is not a method which can be recommended for most people.

SCORING AND RECORDING

Most targets are divided into scoring rings with their value decreasing outwards from ten at the centre to one at the outer ring. Some targets do

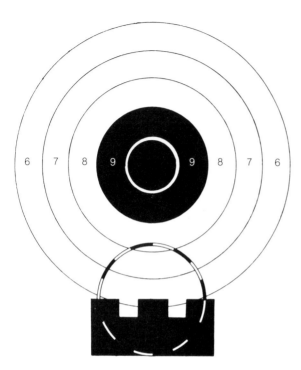

Area of wobble: provided the correct sight picture is maintained, the aim can move anywhere in the dotted circle and you will still score a nine or a ten. This is because there is no angular error, only a parallel error.

not have score rings beyond four. However, not all targets are circular: the international 25-metre rapid-fire target, for example, has vertically elongated lozenge-shaped scoring zones with rounded edges, valued at ten in the middle to six at the outside. Some targets have rectangular scoring zones. The international UIT targets are described and illustrated in *General Technical Rules for All Shooting Disciplines* at rules 3.2 to 3.4c.

To describe where a shot has hit a target, its distance from the centre is measured by its position in the scoring zone. This can be further defined by calling it 'good' or 'bad' depending upon how far out it is from the centre. Thus, a 'good 8' would be near the 9 zone, whilst a 'poor 8' would be near the 7 zone. Shot holes are measured at the outside edge of the hole and

if the hole has touched the line between two scoring zones, the higher value is allowed. Bullet holes in targets close up after the bullet has passed through and the hole is really larger than it appears. In order to measure the exact size of the hole a plug gauge is used. This is accurately made, and must be placed in the bullet hole very carefully so that the true value of the shot may be judged. It helps if a block or board with a hole in it about one inch (2.5 centimetres) in diameter is placed behind the target to support the card around the hole being gauged. Once a hole has been gauged, it cannot be re-gauged with any accuracy. In competition, a hole should therefore only be gauged by the official scorer. A magnifying lens will help you to decide if the gauge is actually touching a score-line. Always view the gauge from directly above, otherwise you may look under the edge of the gauge if you view it from the side.

There is an exception to measuring shot holes at their inner edge, and this occurs with the air pistol ten-metre target. Here, a special outward scoring gauge is used. This has a wide flange and the measurement is made according to the position of the outer edge. Outward scoring is used to give a clearer picture where the scoring rings are close together and within the black aiming mark.

You will find it both useful and interesting to keep a record of your shooting in a score book. You may have to make your own score book to suit your particular requirements. First of all you need a diagram of the target, which can be actual size in the case of the ten-metre air pistol target. Then draw vertical and horizontal lines passing through the centre.

In training you can plot each shot as it is fired. In a match you may find this distracting, so you may prefer to plot your shots after each series, although you can, of course, still plot them after each shot if you wish to do so. This is particularly feasible in the air pistol event where you have to change your target after each shot anyway. However you wish to do it, you will build up a picture of all your shots.

While you are shooting, you enter the score

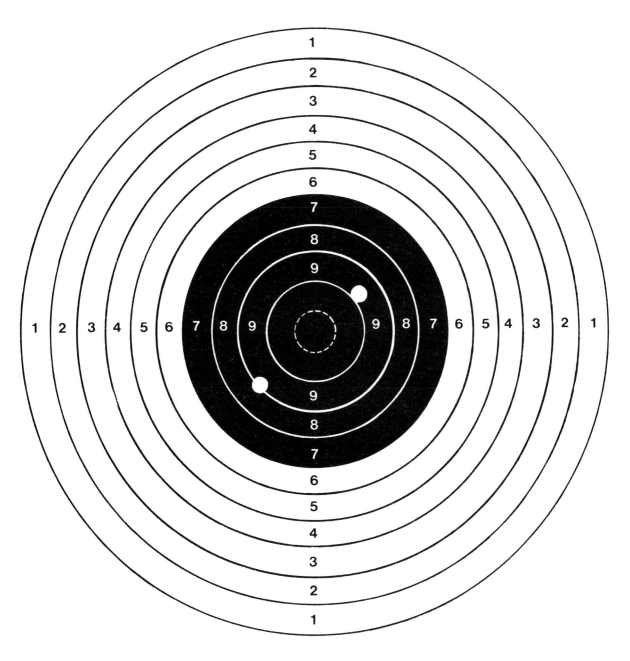

The shot at two o'clock scores ten; while that at seven o'clock scores nine.

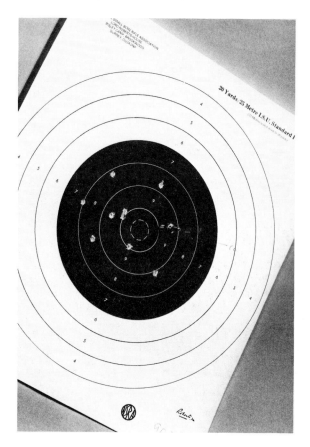

*A .22 gauge in a bullet hole, scoring ten as
its edge touches the demarcation line.*

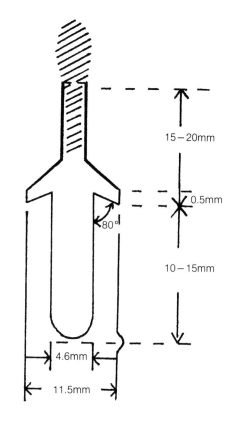

of each shot in the appropriate square in the
matrix. You should also make a note of any
sight alteration you may have made.

After you have completed the course you
may, if you wish, add up each series of ten shots
and write that score to the right of the relevant
line in the matrix. Now you can analyse your
shooting by completing the other sections on the
score-sheet. Your plotting of all your shots on
the target diagram can be confusing, and you
may decide to use more than one diagram for a
60-shot course.

From the total plotting of all your shots you
can see if any sight alteration is needed. This
information will be more obvious if you add up
the number of shots in each quadrant and write
these figures on the 'total distribution' section
of your diagram. Then add up the two left-hand

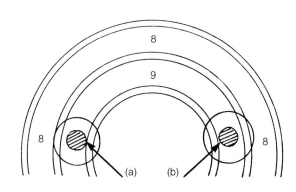

*Use of the 'outward' scoring gauge. (a) shows a
doubtful shot hole with the 'outward' scoring
gauge in place. The outside edge of the flange is
not outside the nine ring and therefore the shot
scores ten. (b) shows another doubtful shot hole:
the 'outward' scoring gauge shows the outside
edge of the flange lying over the nine demarcation
line and into the eight zone, thereby giving a
score of nine.*

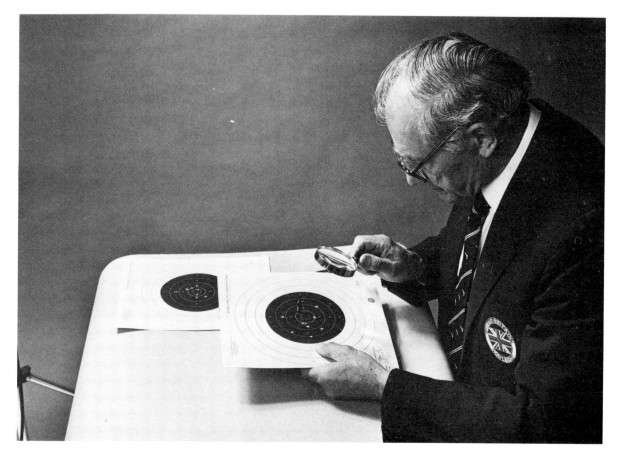

Scoring a target. A board with a hole in it supports the card around the shot hole. The plug gauge is carefully inserted into the shot hole. A magnifying lens helps to make fine judgement more accurate.

quadrants and write this total to the left of the short vertical line. Similarly add up the two right-hand quadrants and write this total to the right of the line. Deal likewise with the high and low shots, writing the totals above and below the short horizontal line.

Count the number of tens you have in each quadrant and write these figures in the corresponding quadrants on your 'ten' diagram showing distribution by scoring rings. Repeat this process for all the other scoring rings. It may well be that the total shot distribution indicated that you should alter your sights, perhaps to the left, to centre your group on the scoring rings; but this last analysis will show

that if you did move your group to the left, you would move your tens and nines away from their scoring rings. Thus your problem in this instance is not to alter your sights, but to examine your poorer shots to discover why they have pulled your total group out to the right. This is one of the values of analysing your shots by score rings.

There is one more way in which you can increase your pleasure from shooting. So far we have recorded the actual score of each shot and the total score for the course of fire, or parts of it. Of course total scores are important, although they can be distracting too, especially during a match. What really matters is that you

Date: _____   Place: _____   Remarks:

FEINWERKBAU 65 / No 4231
ELEY MATCH PELLETS : SERIAL P8240
LIGHT RATHER DIM

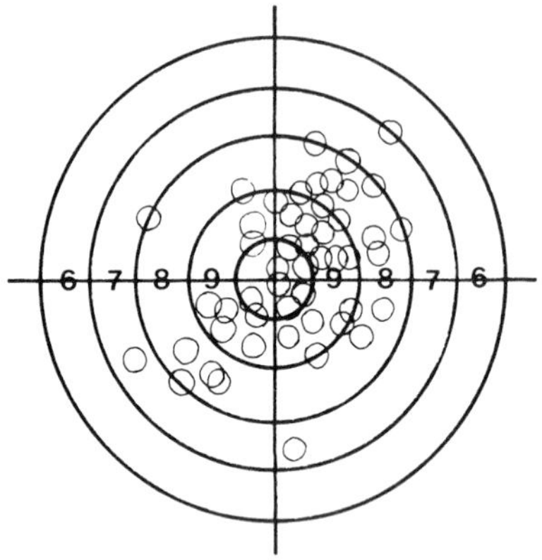

Target	Shots					Score
Sighters	8	9	8	10	10	45
Sighters	9	7	8	9	9	42
	10	9	8	9	8	44
	10	9	9	8	8	44
	9	8	10	7	9	43
	9	8	8	9	10	44
	7	9	9	9	8	42
	8	9	8	9	9	43
	8	9	9	10	10	46
	9	8	8	10	10	45
Total						351

Total distribution

```
   4 | 24
  ----+----      15 | 35      28
  11 | 11                     22
```

Distribution by scoring rings

```
        1 | 4            2 | 10
  10  ----+----     9  ----+----
        2 | 3            4 | 5

        1 | 9            – | 1
  8   ----+----     7  ----+----
        4 | 2            1 | 1

        – | –            – | –
  6   ----+----     5  ----+----
        – | –            – | –
```

Total number of:

10's — 10 = 20%
9's — 21 = 42%
8's — 16 = 32%
7's — 3 = 6%
6's — = %
5's — = %

A record and analysis book made up for ten-metre air pistol shooting.

improve your performance. If you now add up how many tens you shot and convert this to a percentage of the number of shots you fired, and enter these figures in the places provided, you will have another way of looking at your achievement. Similarly, add up each of the other score values and enter them as total figures and as percentages. Now you will see clearly how a few bad shots may have pulled down your total score and you can concentrate your attention on eliminating your poorer shots. Thus, as well as looking at your total score for each session, you can look at the percentages of its component parts and, hopefully, derive satisfaction from seeing these percentages getting better each time.

To be fully useful, any score book or sheet must show when and where you shot the series or competition; what the weather or light conditions were; whether you felt tired or well; what ammunition you used, recording both the make and batch number; the time you took to complete the course; which pistol you used, and so forth. You can record these matters under the 'remarks' section. You can also show here where you made sight alterations.

Quite apart from the useful and interesting information your score book will build up over a period, there is another benefit from maintaining a score book in this fashion. In slow-fire shooting you will enter the position and value of each shot as you see it through your telescope immediately after you have fired it (unless you choose not to do this in a match). This will not only help you to relax, but will also slow down your rate of fire, giving your body more time in which to restore its oxygen level and help to prepare your concentration for your next shot. In any competition you should always treat each shot as a separate match. Pay attention to a group drifting away from centre, but disregard the score it may be making. What has been shot is finished; think only of your technique in firing the shot which lies in the barrel. Remember, a good score is made not so much by firing excellent shots as by eliminating the bad shots.

Obviously in rapid-fire, timed-fire and duelling shoots you will not be able to plot each individual shot as it is fired. Here you will have to record such details as you can after each five-shot series.

CLOTHING AND FOOTWEAR

If you want to succeed in competitive pistol shooting you will do well to give some thought to the clothes you will wear. Your actual choice will be influenced by the type of shooting you are going to do. Obviously you will wear different clothes if you are shooting an air pistol in a warm sports hall from those you would wear on a cold outdoor range exposed to wind and rain. However, your clothes should always be comfortable and should not restrict your shooting arm and shoulder. Beware of a jacket which does not give freedom of movement across the shoulders; you do not want your non-shooting arm having any effect upon your shooting arm.

Bad weather clothing: note the fabric cover enclosing the fingers and hand, but clear of the wrist so that no support is given to it. Cold weather, often coupled with wet and wind, can cause loss of sensitivity to free pistol shooters' fingers – as well as this cover, the shooter will need a hand warmer in his pocket.

Make sure your clothes allow a good air circulation around your body, and that they do not restrict any blood vessels.

If you are shooting out of doors you will need some lightweight showerproof outer garment, preferably with a hood, to keep you dry from head to toes. In bad weather you will need some form of outer parka to keep you warm when not actually shooting. Do not forget your gloves, and hand-warmer, for if your hands get cold you soon lose sensitivity in your fingers.

Do not be tempted to combine shooting with sunbathing! This can be dangerous and will certainly not help your shooting: dangerous because ejected cartridge cases are very hot and can burn your arm or any other part they touch. For this reason alone do not wear an open-necked shirt – there is nothing more upsetting than getting your neighbour's empty case down your chest when you are on aim. Another bad effect of shooting with an exposed arm is that the hairs on your arm will sense even slight breezes and make you think the wind is stronger than it is. This can cause your subconscious to make you aim off 'for wind'.

Proper footwear is important. Your shoes or boots should support your ankles, keep your feet dry, allow good blood circulation and allow your toes room in which to move and the freedom to grip the ground. When it comes to your socks there really is no substitute for wool, as it keeps your feet dry and ventilated.

Ladies need to pay particular attention to their choice of footwear if they are accustomed to wearing high heels, since they will have altered the foot, ankle and calf muscles. They will need to train these muscles to be steady and comfortable in lower-heeled shoes.

There is much to be said for having a smart outfit to wear. It will help you to feel better, and give you just that little bit of added confidence if you know you look the part. A tracksuit is a suitable garment for all forms of pistol shooting, but it may be necessary to modify it by inserting trouser pockets so that you can restrain your non-shooting hand in the most suitable place.

If you decide to buy a pistol shooting jacket, make sure that it conforms to the UIT rules and the advice just given. It should support your non-shooting hand in the correct place so that your shoulders can remain level, without strain across the back of the jacket. Leather does not stretch like wool, so a correct fit is very important.

One essential item, which can be called clothing, is your ear protection. Pistol shooting is particularly harmful to your hearing, as gases are still burning (exploding) as they leave the short barrel, causing dangerously high noise levels. You must wear either ear-muffs or ear-plugs, or even both together, all the time you are shooting or near shooting. Even if there are no explosions, it is still a good idea to wear your ear protectors, for example when shooting an air pistol, as they help to reduce noises which would otherwise be distracting.

FAULT ANALYSIS

Each individual shooter's eyesight and hold are different so that the first time you shoot with a pistol, it is very unlikely that your shots will be grouped around the centre of the target. This does not matter, as the sights can be altered to centre your group of shots on the target. Once you have gained sufficient experience to be able to fire your shots in a reasonable group, you can analyse your results and take action accordingly. Errors will be apparent either by the group shifting, or by odd shots striking the target away from the group. There can be three different causes for errors:

1. Fault in pistol or ammunition.
2. Errors in the shooter's performance.
3. Changes in weather or light conditions.

Faulty Pistol or Ammunition

A common source of random error is a sight becoming loose on the pistol, or the sight adjustment screws working loose. The obvious remedy is to ensure that all holding screws (not adjustment screws) are tightly secured before you start to shoot. Use a screwdriver that is right for the job: too small or too weak a screwdriver will cause damage to your pistol through burring the slot in the screw's head. Make sure that the screws holding the grips and any barrel weights to the frame are tight, because they too can cause a random error if they are loose.

If you have stripped the pistol down, make sure that it has been reassembled correctly. For instance, it is possible to replace the barrel on a Hi-Standard Citation in such a way that the barrel is not aligned with the frame. It will still function, but the bullets will go very high.

Errors in any one direction can be caused by a bright spot on the corner of the sights, so make sure you have blackened your sights before shooting.

If the barrel contains a build-up of lead in the rifling grooves, this will restrict the bullet's travel. Eventually it will reach a point where the next bullet up the barrel will push the lead out on its nose. This results in the shot going high, and you will notice that the hole looks larger and is surrounded with a black ring, rather as if a wad-cutter had been used. This is caused by the bullet being delayed in the barrel as it forces the lead out, so the gases build up more than the usual pressure, resulting in more recoil. The larger hole and black ring are caused by the lead carried on the bullet's nose.

Should the ammunition be faulty, the shot will usually go low due to a reduced propellant. Normally you will hear a different report, either louder or softer than usual. Occasionally you may get what is called a 'hang fire', which is more likely in centre-fire ammunition. Here the primer does not burn as it should, and there can be a measurable delay between the igniter being struck and the main charge detonating. For this reason, if you have a misfire, keep your pistol pointing in a safe direction for a second or two until you are sure a hang fire has not occurred.

Always look at your ammunition before you load it to see that there is no obvious defect, such as a build-up of grease on the nose, or some damage to the bullet or case. Any such defect will disturb the bullet's flight. Air pistol pellets are particularly critical in this respect because they travel relatively slowly and are quite soft. Make sure that the skirt and the head are not damaged. These are the two areas of the pellet which touch the barrel and which pick up the spin from the rifling. If for any reason they are not in perfect contact with the barrel, the pellet's flight will be impaired. Always shoot a match with a batch of pellets you have tested, as you will find the ballistics vary from batch to batch. This is partly caused by the oxidation of the alloy from which they are made, which makes the pellet skirt less pliable so it does not open out into the rifling properly.

Errors in Performance

Do not try to assess errors or make alterations to your sights on less than four or five shots, which should have been good releases and not 'scoped. If you are a beginner then do not alter your sights on the results of less than ten shots. If you make alterations on the results of two or three shots, there is a risk of chasing your shots, especially if you are spotting each shot with your telescope after it has been fired.

1. *Grip*: if you do not hold the pistol tight enough it will bounce around in your hand as it recoils, giving high errors, usually to the right (for a right-handed person). If you hold the pistol too tightly, you will induce tremor which could result in random errors. It is likely that you will experience random errors if you alter the pressure of your grip from shot to shot. Your grip must be consistent throughout your shooting.

If you allow the ball of the hand to put pressure on to the grip you will cause a high right error. The remedy is to concentrate on taking the correct grip, so that the pistol is held between the second and third fingers and the base of the thumb.

If you have a horizontal group, and are sure your trigger control was correct, then a possible cause of such an error could be an incorrect grip. Take your grip again, trying to ensure you do it properly and seeing that the pistol points well, that is, that the foresight comes naturally into the middle of the rearsight notch without you having to bend your wrist. If you find that you do have to bend your wrist, then either your hold on the pistol is wrong or the grips are not right for your hand and will need modification.

2. *Cant*: cant is the tipping of the pistol to one side so that the top of the rearsight is no longer horizontal. Some experts say that a little cant does not matter, as your sight adjustment will compensate for any error. However, we do not believe this is true and advise you to eliminate cant whenever it occurs. Unless you watch for it, you may be unaware that you are canting

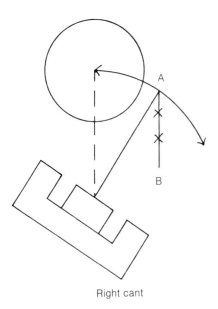

Right cant

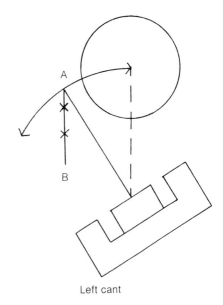

Left cant

The effect of cant. Depending upon the degree of cant and the distance to the target, the bullet will strike somewhere along the line A – B.

your pistol, but your coach should quickly notice it. If you cant a pistol to the left, your shots will group to the left and a little low. One of the problems with cant is that it is seldom consistent and will usually increase during a shoot as you begin to tire, so mere sight alteration will not counter its effect. If you feel that it is really uncomfortable for you to hold your pistol vertically for any length of time, it is likely that your grips need adjustment so that the pistol will sit vertically in your hand when your hand and wrist are in their natural position.

3. *Trigger control*: signs that your trigger control is not correct may appear as shots grouped low left (for a right-handed person). This may occur if your trigger finger is touching the side of the frame. Low shots to the right or left could be caused by snatching the trigger.

If you have occasional shots hitting the target at three o'clock, you may be pushing your trigger; conversely, shots at nine o'clock show that you may be pulling it. The remedy in either case is for you to shoot at a blank card;

concentrate on squeezing the trigger straight to the rear, with the centre of the first pad of your trigger finger pressing squarely on the trigger at the moment of let-off. Imagine that you are pulling the foresight back through the rearsight notch.

Another error closely associated with trigger control may be called 'riding the recoil'. This happens as the shot breaks, when you allow the pistol, especially its muzzle, to rise, resulting in a gross error at 12 o'clock. Good trigger control – the surprise break – and good follow-through should eliminate this error which is related to anticipating the let-off.

4. *Sight picture*: if the foresight is to the left of the centre of the notch in the rearsight, an angular error to the left will result, and such an error will be large. Similarly, if the top of the foresight is above the level of the top of the rearsight, an angular error at 12 o'clock will occur. There can be no exception to the sight picture being absolutely correct at the moment of let-off. Angular errors cannot be tolerated.

5. *Aim*: errors in aiming may be acceptable if

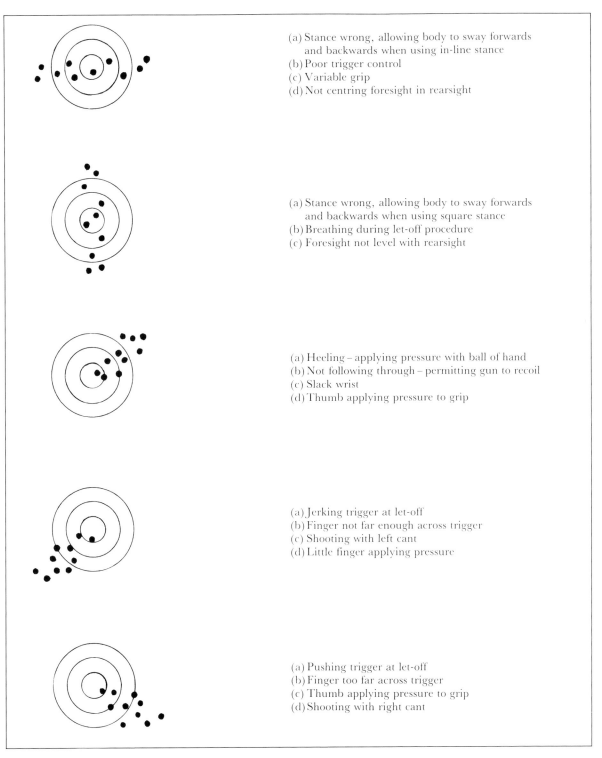

(a) Stance wrong, allowing body to sway forwards and backwards when using in-line stance
(b) Poor trigger control
(c) Variable grip
(d) Not centring foresight in rearsight

(a) Stance wrong, allowing body to sway forwards and backwards when using square stance
(b) Breathing during let-off procedure
(c) Foresight not level with rearsight

(a) Heeling – applying pressure with ball of hand
(b) Not following through – permitting gun to recoil
(c) Slack wrist
(d) Thumb applying pressure to grip

(a) Jerking trigger at let-off
(b) Finger not far enough across trigger
(c) Shooting with left cant
(d) Little finger applying pressure

(a) Pushing trigger at let-off
(b) Finger too far across trigger
(c) Thumb applying pressure to grip
(d) Shooting with right cant

Fault analysis.

they are within the area of tolerance you have set yourself. You can move anywhere in an area the size of the ten ring and as long as the sight picture is correct (and no other error occurs) you will still get a ten. This is because the line of fire is parallel to the line of sight – if your pistol is 1/10in (2.5mm) to one side, the bullet too will travel along a path 1/10in (2.5mm) from the centre line and will strike the target 1/10in (2.5mm) from its centre. Errors in aiming can occur in any direction and will therefore be random.

6. *Breathing*: if you fail to control your breathing and do not hold your breath while releasing the shot, you will have high and/or low errors.

7. *Holding on aim too long*: if you hold on aim too long, you will shoot random errors because all or any of the above faults may occur as your ability to maintain optimum concentration begins to fail. The worst feature of this fault is that it will almost certainly include an element of angular sighting error, because your brain will be affected by the lack of oxygen in your blood, causing your vision to suffer.

8. *Mind wander*: mind wander or mind drift means that you lose your concentration as you start to think about extraneous matters. This is more likely when you are already tired, perhaps after a hard day's work, or if you have some domestic problem worrying you. Mind wander will cause random errors, as your loss of concentration could affect any or all of the factors involved in firing a well-released shot. The way to regain your concentration is explained in Chapter 4.

Changes in Light or Weather Conditions

1. *Indoor lighting*: if you are shooting close to a side wall on an indoor range, you may find that the reflected light from the wall can cause your shots to group to that side. You will need to alter your sights accordingly. Your sighting series of shots should show you by how much you must alter your windage. This is just one reason why you should always take just as much care in firing your sighting series as you take with your match shots. Sighters are not throw-away shots to warm up the barrel. Use them for what they are intended – to assess conditions.

You will usually find that you will need to alter your elevation when changing from outdoor daylight to indoor artificial light. This is because the intensity of the light changes and makes the white between the aiming mark and your sight top appear to be of different depth.

2. *Outdoor light*: if you are shooting outdoors you must watch the light closely. If clouds obscure the sun after it has been shining you will need to lower your rearsight. Conversely, if the sun comes out after it has been dull you will need to raise your elevation. The rule is 'light up – sights up'.

Changes in light alter the appearance of the depth of the white gap you have between the top of your foresight and the bottom of the black aiming mark. If no correction is made this will result in a vertically elongated group of shots. If clouds are frequently scudding across the sky it may be better to watch the approaching shadow coming over the ground and take aim when conditions are even, rather than constantly altering your sights.

3. *Wind effects*: in really windy conditions you are advised to brace yourself rather more than you would normally, by placing your feet wider apart. The wind's effect on the bullet will be less than its effect on your extended arm. If you are shooting in a strong cross-wind at 50 metres you will need to alter the windage on your rearsight, but the amount it would blow the bullet sideways is relatively small, whereas the disturbance to your gun arm can be considerable. Watch for gusts of wind coming by observing grass, flags or trees and try to shoot between the gusts. Do not hold on aim too long hoping for calmer conditions – that is a great mistake. Much better that you shoot quickly when you judge the wind to be steady; build up the pressure on your trigger more quickly than you would do normally.

If the wind is coming from your front, you may find it helpful to lean into it a little. The converse is not so helpful!

If the weather is warm, you may be tempted

to shoot with a bare arm. Do not do this. Besides the risk of being burnt by an empty cartridge case, the hairs on your arm will detect the slightest breeze, thus distracting your attention.

PISTOL TYPES

The word 'pistol' includes all types of hand gun, and embraces revolvers, single-shot pistols, semi-automatic or self-loading pistols and air or gas-operated pistols. Their design and calibres vary considerably from a centre-fire pistol with a calibre of .455 to an air pistol of .177 calibre. Whole books could be written to describe this vast range and, indeed, there are many books available which deal in detail with the construction and operation of pistols. Here we are concerned with how to shoot pistols, rather than with their history and manufacture.

Revolvers

Revolvers are made in calibres ranging from .22 to .455. In a revolver, the cartridges are held in a cylinder; as the hammer is moved into its cocked position, either through the action of pulling the trigger, or by pulling the cocking spur back, the cylinder is rotated to align the next chamber with the breech. One common feature is that the trigger operates through a sear to release the hammer. This is then driven forward by a spring to strike the detonator in the cartridge.

This type of mechanism is inherently slow to operate – there is a small delay (known as the lock time) between the trigger release and the bullet leaving the cartridge, and a further delay

The Smith & Wesson K – 22 Masterpiece revolver (Model No. 17). This is made with 4-inch, 6-inch or 8-inch barrels. The cylinder is chambered for six .22 long rifle cartridges. The rearsight is adjustable for elevation and windage.

Smith & Wesson Model No.629. This .44 Magnum revolver is made with either 4-inch, 6-inch or 8⅜-inch barrels (here seen with 8⅜-inch). It has a micrometer click adjustable rearsight. The cylinder holds six rounds.

Some of Smith & Wesson's extensive range of revolvers (top to bottom): Model No.25–5, a .45 Colt; Model No. 57, a .41 Magnum; Model No. 27, a .357 Magnum.

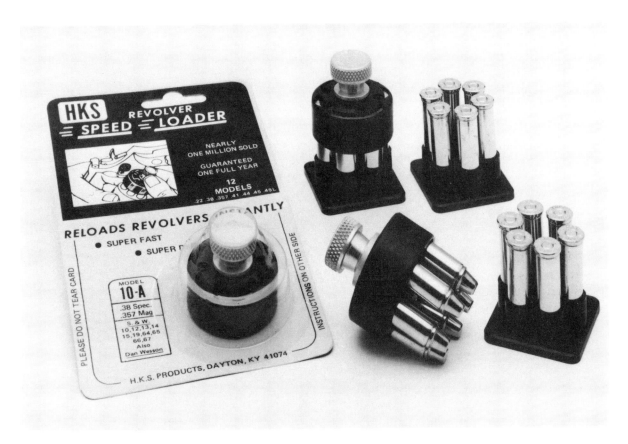

Speed loaders, with a block to hold the ammunition from which to reload the speed loader quickly. These are made in sizes to handle cartridges from .22 to .44 Magnum, for ten makes of revolver.

while the bullet travels along the barrel. During this time you must endeavour to keep the pistol steady. One advantage of a revolver is that the design allows the butt angle to be such that your wrist can be bent down and locked in a steady position. This gives good control of the grip. A revolver also sits very low in the hand, allowing the recoil to be transmitted straight back into the hand and arm with very little deflection at the muzzle. Another advantage is that once the hammer has fallen, there are no moving parts to disturb the bullet's trajectory as it moves along the barrel.

There are three different ways in which revolvers can be opened, be it for loading or inspection. The usual way is for a catch to be released which enables the cylinder to be swung out of the frame, usually to the left. There are revolvers which 'break' open – on releasing a catch the barrel and cylinder can be swung forwards and down from a hinge on the butt. This action automatically ejects any cartridges in the cylinder. In the third type, the cylinder remains attached to the frame, but its rear is enclosed, except for a 'gate'. This gate has to be opened to eject the cartridge case and to reload another round, chamber by chamber, as the cylinder is rotated to align each chamber with the gate.

Most revolvers have a cylinder containing six chambers. There are devices sold which hold the relevant number of cartridges in a type of clip so that you can load the six chambers in one operation. These devices are called 'speed loaders', and are of particular use in Practical Pistol shooting.

Semi-automatic Pistols

All semi-automatic pistols contain the cartridges in a magazine which is loaded into the pistol. The breech-block (sometimes called the 'slide') is driven to the rear by the explosion of the first cartridge and as it moves back, the extractor removes the now empty case from the breech. An ejector then flicks the case out of the pistol. As the breech-block moves back it compresses a spring which eventually drives it forwards again; and it also re-cocks the trigger mechanism. As it moves forwards it takes the next round from the lips of the magazine and feeds it into the breech. The pistol is then ready to be fired again.

The semi-automatic pistol is convenient for most forms of competitive shooting as it will fire single shots in rapid succession each time you release the trigger, without you having to recock it. Designs vary considerably. Some contain the magazine in the butt, inserted from below, while others have it inserted from the top. Some have the magazine below the barrel but in front of the trigger guard, with the magazine being inserted from below, while in others of a similar type it is inserted from above. These designs have different centres of gravity and you should choose a pistol whose balance suits you. In addition, the grip angle relative to the line of the barrel in the vertical plane varies. Some are almost at 90 degrees (known as a military grip), while others have a more oblique angle. Here again it is a matter of trying as many different models as possible to find those which suit your hand and physique.

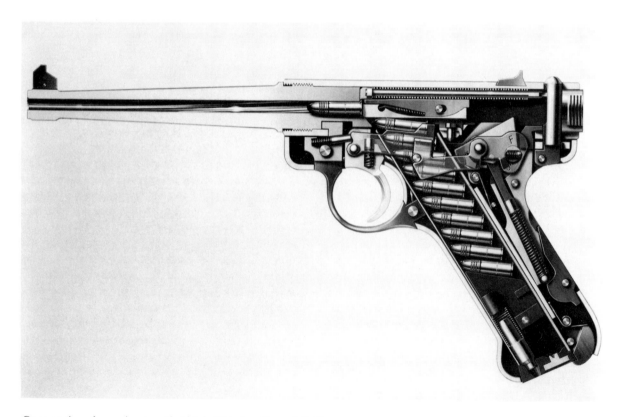

Cross-section of a semi-automatic pistol. This is a Ruger Mk II, unusually shown with ten rounds in the magazine and an eleventh in the breech.

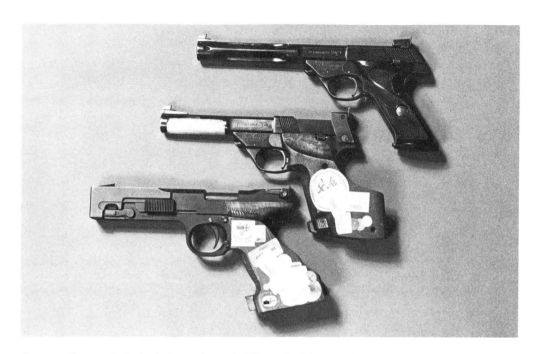

Some popular standard pistols (top to bottom): Hi-standard Supermatic Citation, with a 7-inch barrel and factory-issue grips; Hi-Standard Supermatic Citation with 5-inch bull barrel and anatomical grips; FAS.

The Britarms Mk 3 – note how the trigger is mounted on a shaft, along which it can be moved, to alter the trigger position in the fore and aft line.

Smith & Wesson target pistols (top to bottom): Model No. 41, a .22 here seen with a 7-inch barrel; Model No. 41 fitted with a 5½-inch heavy barrel; Model No. 52, a .38 Master.

Single-shot Pistols

These are of two types: very specialised free pistols designed for the Olympic-type 50-metre match and standard single-shot pistols for other slow-fire shooting. Some have a bolt action and others use the Martini falling-block type of action.

Free pistols are delicate pieces of machinery intended to fire with the greatest accuracy. The novice would be ill-advised to invest in one until he has mastered a standard slow-fire pistol. The free pistol is discussed in detail in Chapter 3.

The standard single-shot pistol – such as the Webley, the Hämmerli 120, or the Jurek – is useful for a beginner. Because only one round can be loaded at a time, it is safer to use than a semi-automatic pistol. Furthermore, as there are no moving parts except the trigger and hammer, it is easily understood. While special single-shot pistols with large calibres do exist for the long-range shooter, the vast majority of pistols are made in .22 calibre.

Air and CO_2 Pistols

Here we will only describe the recoil-less air and gas-operated pistols, as the competitive pistol shooter really has no need for the recoiling types. However, so that our story is complete, you may wish to know that air pistols are made in .22 as well as .177 calibre, and some of the former are fitted with telescopic sights. They are not permitted in competitive shooting, nor should you allow them to be used on your range because the kinetic energy available with the larger pellets can damage the pellet catchers used for match shooting.

Recoil-less .177 air pistols obtain their energy from air forced out of a cylinder by a piston, which is itself driven forward by a spring. The spring is compressed by the action of a cocking lever. Usually considerable force is needed to operate this lever. In some pistols the lever is located at the side (as in the Feinwerkbau models 65, 80 and 90), in some the trigger guard forms the lever (Walther LP3) while others make use of the barrel (Original model 10) or an extension of the barrel (FAS) to cock the spring.

CO_2 or gas-operated pistols have a cylinder of compressed gas, usually in liquid form, lying under the barrel which is sufficient for about 300 shots. The CO_2 pistol has some advantages over the air pistol. Firstly, you do not have to cock a spring for each shot, so you save considerable exertion in the course of a 60-shot match preceded by perhaps 15 sighting shots. Secondly, the power available is greater and so the pellet travels faster. This gives it a flatter trajectory, but what is more important is that it leaves the barrel sooner after trigger release and so reduces the risk of its flight being disturbed by you moving the pistol while the pellet is travelling along the barrel.

A new trigger guard provides more space. The trigger tongue length is variable over a range of 17mm. The Hammerli 208 s also has easily changed rearsight elements, and a 200g barrel weight.

The SIG 210 – 5 with a 150mm barrel. Normally in 9mm or 7.65mm calibre there is a .22 conversion kit available to reduce training costs.

Smith & Wesson Model No.645, a .45 calibre semi-automatic pistol with a 5-inch barrel. It has fixed sights with a radius of 6⅝ inches. The magazine holds eight rounds.

Ruger Mk II with Bull barrel and micrometer adjustable sights.

Ruger Mk II with stainless-steel barrel and adjustable rearsight.

Because of the power available in a CO_2 pistol the Home Office in Great Britain has decreed that you must apply to the police for permission to own one, and it has to be entered on your Firearms Certificate.

Feinwerkbau make a junior version of their Model 2 CO_2 pistol which is lighter and therefore easier for young shooters to handle. It has a shorter barrel and a smaller CO_2 cylinder, which holds sufficient gas for 200 shots, instead of 300 shots with the senior model.

Some people do not understand how the cylinders for a CO_2 pistol are refilled. It is not difficult, but as with so many other things you must be careful. CO_2 (carbon dioxide) is a gas which changes to a liquid when it is compressed; the warmer it is, the more pressure will be needed to make that change. To find out how much CO_2 there is in a cylinder you must weigh the cylinder. The manufacturer will have told you in the handbook what is the weight of an empty cylinder, and what weight of CO_2 you may add. The manufacturer also supplies unions (nuts) which will enable the cylinder to be fitted to more common sources of bulk CO_2.

Having weighed your cylinder to see how much CO_2 is needed to fill it, you must cool your cylinder so that it can receive the liquid CO_2 without raising its temperature to the point where it will boil off and become gaseous. Either put it in a freezer for an hour, or, if you still have some CO_2 in it, you can use the tool provided with the pistol to bleed off some CO_2, which will have the effect of instantly chilling the cylinder.

Now connect it to your supply cylinder, open the valve and turn the main cylinder upside-down to let the liquid CO_2 flow into your pistol cylinder. This will only take half a minute. It is advisable to wear thick gloves when doing this, in case your skin sticks to the freezing metal, or is exposed to a stream of very cold gas. Then shut the main valve, turn the supply cylinder upright again and disconnect the pistol cylinder. Finally weigh it to see that it has taken in the full load of liquid CO_2.

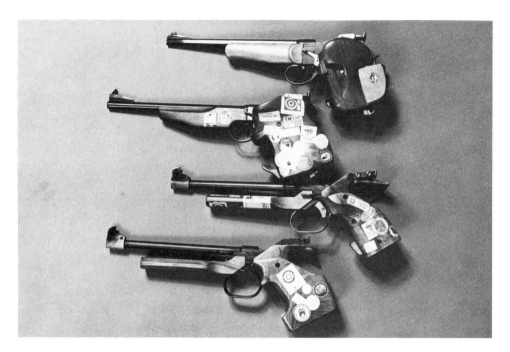

Some popular free pistols (top to bottom): Hammerli 102; TOZ 35; Hammerli 150; Hammerli 152.

Some popular air pistols (top to bottom): Feinwerkbau 80; Feinwerkbau 65; Feinwerkbau CO$_2$; Air Match (with extended foresight).

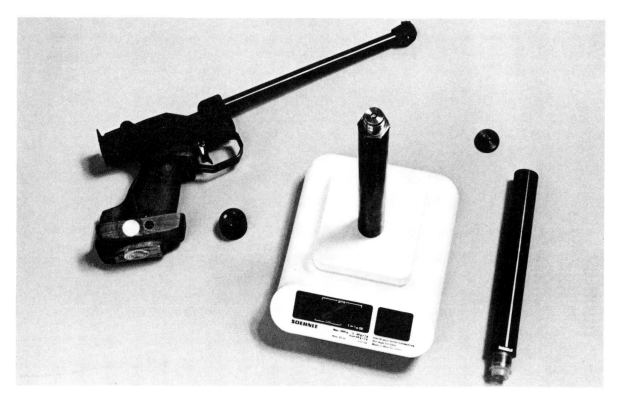

Weighing a CO_2 cylinder to discover its contents. Note the damping weight has been removed from the cylinder. The bleeding tool is between the pistol and the scales.

CHOOSING A PISTOL

Your choice of pistol will be governed by three factors:

1. The type of shooting you wish to do.
2. How much you can afford to pay.
3. Your physique.

Type of Shooting

Once the rudiments have been mastered with a single-shot pistol, unless you wish to specialise in slow-fire events from the start, you will probably find what you want among the semi-automatic pistols.

A semi-automatic pistol, or self or auto-loader as they are sometimes called, can be used to fire single shots. Thus you can shoot several different disciplines with it. The small-bore ones are made to take two types of .22 cartridge; these are the .22 short and the .22 long rifle. Pistols chambered for short cartridges are used only in the UIT rapid-fire event and are rather special pistols. As a beginner you will find the type chambered for the long rifle cartridge more useful.

If your inclination lies in full-bore shooting, known also as centre fire, you will have the choice of buying a revolver or a semi-automatic pistol. The latter is more versatile, due to the speed with which successive shots can be fired. You will also have to choose which calibre you are going to use, and here the cost of ammunition will probably be a factor to consider. Centre-fire pistols are available in calibres ranging from .32 to .455, although more usually the .45 is the largest calibre you are likely to meet.

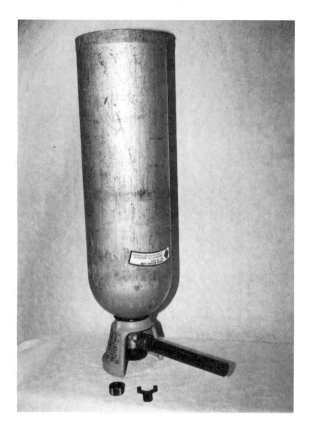

Filling a pistol's gas cylinder with liquid CO_2 from a 14lb cylinder. In front is the special spanner, and the tool for bleeding the pistol's cylinder prior to refilling it, in order to cool it to a temperature at which the liquid CO_2 will not change to gas.

Competitive pistol shooting is a precise art, so you will need a pistol with a rearsight that can be altered to allow for changes in elevation and windage (as the sideways alteration is known). Most organisations' rules stipulate various parameters covering pistol design, and one of these is that the sight base must not exceed 10in (254mm) for centre-fire pistols (UIT rule 4.4c); another states that the length of the barrel must not exceed 6in (153mm) (UIT rule 4.4b). So you should know the rules before you venture out to buy your own pistol; better still, take a copy of the rule book with you.

If you intend only to shoot slow-fire events, you may choose from a range of single-shot pistols, but here, as with other pistols, make sure that the trigger weight is adjustable and that it is capable of lifting 1kg in Great Britain or 2lb in the USA, or choose a free pistol. The free pistol is a very specialised discipline and you would be well advised to start by using a normal, even conventional, single-shot .22 pistol.

Cost

The prices of new pistols vary very considerably, but generally you get what you pay for, and if a pistol is looked after properly it should maintain its value. If price is a constraint, look at second-hand pistols. They can represent good value and are recommended to someone just starting in the sport who may not wish to invest too much money until they are sure of the type of pistol with which they will be happy.

If you decide to buy a second-hand pistol it is advisable to take an experienced pistol shooter along with you, to help you choose one which is in good mechanical condition.

Physique

Choose a pistol which suits your physique. Pistols are made in many weights and styles, even in one calibre, and you should try as many as possible before deciding which suits your build and strength. How a pistol will 'sit' in your hand varies and what will suit one person will not necessarily please another. Consider the size of the grips. Grips come in small, medium and large sizes, so ensure you are comfortable. You may choose either right-hand or left-hand grips; most manufacturers provide both, but you may have to place a special order for left-handed ones.

MAINTENANCE

If a pistol is properly maintained it should not depreciate much in value. However, there is another reason for paying careful attention to proper maintenance. While the rules for most timed and rapid-fire shooting do accommodate what are called 'allowable' malfunctions, a malfunction can never be to your advantage in a competition. Careful maintenance will help to ensure that you do not suffer one when shooting.

You should buy one of the several proprietary pistol cleaning kits at the start of your shooting, so that you have the correct equipment with which to clean and protect your pistol. How you clean a pistol will depend upon the type you shoot. Modern propellants and primers used in rim-fire cartridges cause very little corrosion, whereas those in centre-fire cartridges may cause considerable fouling.

Air Pistols

Generally, air pistols require very little maintenance, and too much oiling of some parts can even cause trouble. After each shoot you should wipe the external surfaces with a flannelette which has a little anti-corrosive on it, to wipe away any acids from your sweaty fingers. After every 1,000 pellets, pass a soft bristle brush through the barrel to remove any lead deposits.

Parker-Hale pistol-cleaning outfits for .45, .38 and .22 (outfits are made for other calibres). Each box contains an acetate-covered cleaning rod (to protect the barrel from wear), Young's cleaner and rust preventer, gun oil, a jag, a phosphor-bronze brush and cut patches.

Be very careful doing this. Normally a barrel should be cleaned by pushing the cleaning brush or jag in from the breech and out at the muzzle. This is to prevent the cleaning rod, or any other metal part, damaging the rifling near the muzzle, as this is a critical part for imparting spin to the bullet or pellet. With most air pistols it is not easy to strip the barrel from the frame to enable you to clean it in this direction. You may therefore need to push the cleaning rod in from the muzzle, but do be careful not to allow the brush's centre, or the rod, to touch the sides of the barrel when doing so.

A safer, but less effective, way of cleaning an air pistol barrel is to fire a cleaning pellet through it. You can buy these felt pellets, which are made especially for this purpose. When you do this, make sure that your pistol is pointing in a safe direction, as even a felt pellet could cause damage.

If you are going to leave your air pistol for several weeks, it is advisable to pass an oily patch up the barrel, or soak a felt pellet in oil and shoot it through. If you do protect the barrel with oil, remember to clean the oil out by using a dry patch or a dry felt pellet before you shoot it. If you fail to do this, it is possible that the pellet will compress the oil in the rifling and cause a small explosion from the 'diesel' effect. 'Dieselling' can affect all types of pistol.

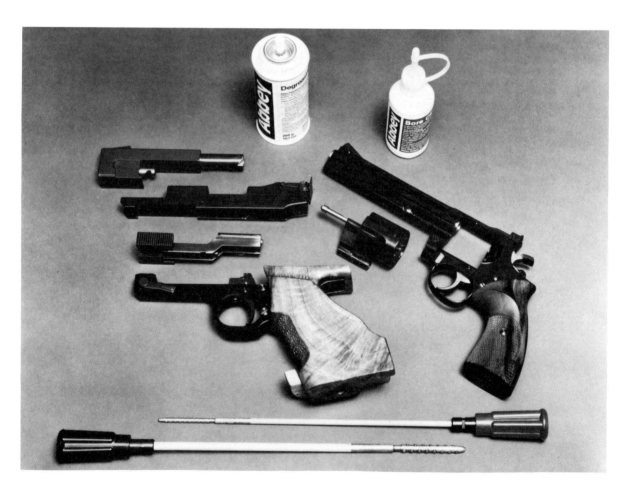

Pistols 'field stripped' ready for cleaning and lubrication.

Rim-fire Pistols

Your rim-fire pistol should be cleaned every time you have finished shooting for the day. To do this, the pistol should be partially stripped down. Remove the magazine or cylinder, remove the barrel (if possible), remove the slide, and in some pistols it may be advisable to remove the grips. As these parts are removed they should be laid on a clean, dry, dust-free surface.

Carefully wipe the surfaces of these parts with a flannelette patch which has been soaked in a cleaning fluid. Change the patch whenever it becomes very dirty.

Soak a patch in a barrel-cleaning fluid, wrap it tightly around the jag and push it through the barrel from the breech end. Repeat this until the fouling is removed. Then use a clean patch which has been soaked in a rust preventive to leave a thin film protecting the barrel. Make sure you do not leave a thick film of fluid or oil in the barrel as this could cause serious damage when the next bullet travels up it.

A child's toothbrush is a good tool with which to clean the faces of the breech and the breech block or slide. Due to the grease with which .22 cartridges are protected, quite a lot of grease will build up on these faces and on the lips of the magazines. Make sure you remove grease and other deposits from behind the extractor and ejector. If the brush does not get it all out, a wooden toothpick or cocktail stick will help you to clean the crevice between the face and the side of the breech block. Make sure the firing pin hole is cleaned. There should now be no

Lubricating the trigger mechanism with Dry-Slide, a lubricant which contains molybdenum disulphide.

visible traces of explosive residue or lead, and you can lubricate the moving surfaces.

Apply a thin film of a good gun oil to the bearing surfaces between the slide and the frame, and move the slide to and fro to work the oil over the two surfaces. Never use more oil than is absolutely necessary, as excess oil will gather dust and grit to itself and form an abrasive compound which will quickly cause wear to the metal surface. Too much oil can cause a gun to jam and can lead to a dangerous build-up of pressure in the breech.

Molybdenum disulphide is used as a lubricant in some preparations, and has the advantage that it builds up a dry, friction-free surface when it has been used for a period of time. But even with this dry lubricant, do not use more than is necessary, and wipe any excess off after you have applied it.

After the moving parts have been lubricated you can reassemble the pistol. Now the external surfaces should be wiped over with a rust inhibitor, such as a silicone gun oil. This can be used on wooden grips as well as the metal parts, and will protect your pistol from fingerprints and moisture.

Centre-fire Pistols

What has been said about cleaning rim-fire pistols applies to centre-fire revolvers and semi-automatic pistols, but, in addition, more attention will have to be given to cleaning powder fouling from the breech and barrel. You will probably find it necessary to use a bronze or brass cleaning brush on the rod, to brush out lead and powder fouling from the barrel before you use a patch on a jag.

Applying Moly G – n paste to the ejector rod.

When cleaning a revolver, pay particular attention to the back of the ejector star and its rod. Make sure that all deposits are removed and that these parts are free of oil. Another place where deposits build up is where the top strap joins the rear of the barrel.

SETTING UP TO SHOOT

Setting up to shoot falls into two parts: the preparation of your equipment and preparing yourself.

Setting up your equipment starts in your home. You should use a shooting box, methodically laid out, to carry all your equipment, with a place for everything, and everything in its place. This way you are not likely to leave something behind. Now check that everything is indeed in its place.

Your equipment can be divided into three categories: those items which are essential, those which are desirable, and those which are optional.

Essential Equipment

First you must check your pistol thoroughly, ensuring it is clean and that all screws are tight (except the trigger adjustment screws). If you have several pistols, make sure that you put into your box those which you will need for the coming match or shoot – this sounds so obvious, but it has been known for a shooter to arrive at the range with the wrong calibre pistol. If it is a semi-automatic, make sure you have sufficient magazines, and that they too are clean and function freely.

Check that you have sufficient ammunition of the correct calibre or calibres. Have extra ammunition to allow for reshoots in the event of malfunction, or tie-breaks and finals. If you are going to shoot a competition and the target stickers have been issued, make sure you have them with you.

Any corrective glasses you wear should also be in the box. Shooting glasses are essential items to protect your eyes from flying

fragments. The last essential item is your ear protection.

With these items you could shoot any match; without any of them you could not really take part. However, you would be at a disadvantage without any of the items in the next category.

Desirable Equipment

Here we include your telescope and stand. See that the lenses are clean and that the stand is serviceable.

Check that you have your stop-watch, and that it is working. Your sight-blacking equipment should be ready for use, topped up with fresh carbide and with a full water compartment. Have a box of matches as a stand-by.

Your cleaning rod or rods and brushes should be in place; a cleaning rod can be useful to clear an empty case stuck in the breech. Check that you have the screwdrivers needed to adjust all screws on your pistol and to alter the sights.

Most ranges require that you have your own bulldog clips with which to fasten your target to the frame. Make sure yours are strong and that you have at least six, to hold your target in a stiff wind. An alternative to fastening your targets with bulldog clips is to staple them to the frame using a staple gun. However, this has the disadvantage that staples will not go into a hardboard back.

Optional Equipment

This includes almost any item which is going to help you to enjoy your shooting: your shooting cap, score book and pen, sight alteration card, appropriate rule book, insect repellant, towel and/or talc, and protective clothing.

Once you arrive at the range, perhaps having passed through weapons control, take your place at the firing line as soon as this is permitted (which should be 15 minutes before you start to shoot). Decide where you are going to stand, and then position your equipment around you in a routine plan, so that you can reach everything you may need without having to move your feet or body. Focus your telescope

Setting up equipment. Note the sight alteration card in the lid of the shooting-glass case, with five rounds of ammunition exposed; a screwdriver, stop-watch, score book and pen are all accessible. There is nothing in front of the pistol. The sight picture reminder is in view.

on the target and check the target number is correct against your firing point number – it can be very confusing if you start off by sighting someone else's shots! Make sure that there is nothing in front of your pistol which might be damaged by an accidental discharge.

PREPARING YOURSELF

Now you are ready to set yourself up to shoot. In a way, your self-preparation will have begun several weeks before, when you began your pre-

match training programme. The fact that you know you have carried out that training conscientiously will give you confidence as you start to set yourself up. This confidence will be enhanced because you know you have studied the rules for the course of fire you are about to shoot and you are completely familiar with the range procedures which will be used. Your confidence will grow from the knowledge that *all* your equipment has been checked and is to hand. This inner confidence is a considerable factor in ensuring that you will enjoy your shoot. The converse is also true. If you have skimped your training, and have just thrown your equipment into your shooting box, you will have a nagging worry in your mind all through the match. This will not only prevent you from applying all your concentration to your shot releases, but will also stop you from enjoying your shooting to the full.

On the day, make sure you arrive at the range with plenty of time to calm down after your journey, especially if you have been driving yourself. Go to the toilet and make yourself comfortable. Carry out your pre-match warm-up of physical exercises to loosen any tight muscles.

Sit down and think the match through. Keep calm. You are in full control of the situation because you have prepared your equipment and yourself for any eventuality. Breathe deeply and relax. Look at the weather or light conditions and plan your shoot accordingly. As the time approaches for you to start the sighting series, think about firing your shot. Visualise the complete aiming and let-off procedure: see yourself launching your shot from a steady hand, see your trigger finger squeezing the trigger directly to the rear in line with the barrel, see the sights correctly aligned, and see the bullet travelling from the pistol into the centre of the target.

3 Types of Shooting

INTERNATIONAL (UIT) SHOOTING

The International Shooting Union is the governing body responsible for shooting in the Olympic Games and World Championships. The initials UIT come from its international name of Union Internationale de Tir. Its rules are contained in two booklets, which are re-published from time to time to incorporate any amendments, so you should ensure that you have the latest copy (the dates are shown on the front covers). The first book is titled *General Technical Rules for all Shooting Disciplines* and covers such matters as safety, range and target standards, the duties of officials, administration, scoring procedures, tie-breaking rules and how to make protests and appeals. The second is *Special Technical Rules* with different editions covering various aspects of the sport. You will need the edition covering free pistol, air pistol, rapid-fire pistol, sport pistol and centre-fire pistol, and standard pistol. This discusses similar areas as the *General Technical Rules*, but goes into precise details for the respective disciplines. If you aspire to shoot in major competitions, you must be familiar with the contents of this book, and with its layout, so that you know where to find a particular matter fairly quickly.

In Chapter 2 the basic principles of pistol shooting were discussed. Here we will cover each of the UIT diciplines and explain how the basic principles need to be modified for each one.

FREE PISTOL

Course of Fire

The Free Pistol match consists of 60 shots, plus an unlimited number of sighting shots, to be fired in two and a half hours at the international precision target, at a distance of 50 metres. The

The popular and successful Hammerli 150 Free Pistol.

The Hammerli 152 has a non-mechanical trigger mechanism.
Squeezing the trigger against an adjustable spring closes a switch which
energises an electric solenoid, so releasing the firing pin, giving a quick
and movement-free link between the trigger release and the firing pin.

Gehmann target changing boxes, showing a target being wound on by
remote control from the firing position.

Free pistol as seen from the front quarter. Note the use of an orthoptic and the non-sighting eye blanked off.

UIT rules permit only five shots to be fired at each target (to make scoring the shots easier), but apart from major championships it is usual to fire ten shots at each target. The sighting shots have to be taken before you start the first competition series.

Modification of Basic Technique

Free pistol shooting is the ultimate in slow-fire precision shooting, and as such it requires the application of all the basic principles to a fine degree. The variations on the basic techniques occur because the match lasts two and a half hours and a free pistol is used. A free pistol does not have to lift any particular trigger weight, so it is usual to have a very light trigger.

Stance

The long duration of the match can be tiring, so any stance which requires considerable muscular effort to maintain it should be avoided. You need to adopt a stance which will help conserve your energy and also one which you can take up easily, so that you can move about between series of shots. You should do this to help relieve muscular strain and to help the body to rid the blood of waste products. You will need to maintain a well-oxygenated blood supply to keep your focus and concentration over the two and a half hours. Leave the firing point from time to time and walk about, breathe deeply, and then relax before resuming your firing position.

It should hardly need saying that in this match you must have a very stable stance, as success depends upon you keeping your pistol very still during the let-off process. A position somewhere between an oblique and an in-line stance will suit most people.

Grip

A consistent, uniform grip must be maintained throughout the match, and to help achieve this

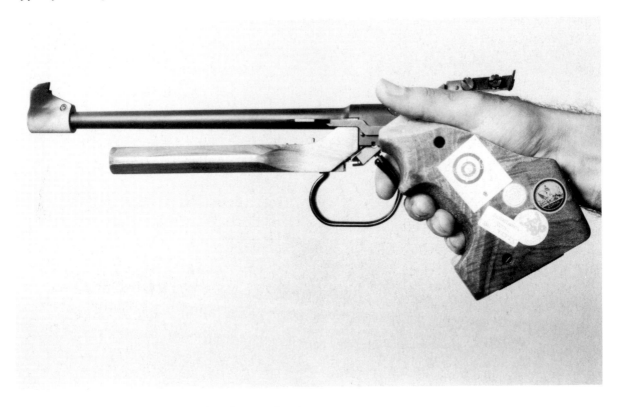

The correct grip – notice the position of the finger on the trigger.

it is usual to have anatomical grips which often encircle the hand, so that you put your hand into them, almost like wearing a glove. Such grips restrict the blood circulation and cause the blood to pool in the hand, making it swell and making the grip too tight. Therefore you must put your pistol down from time to time to allow your blood to regain its normal circulation. Holding your hand above your head will help to restore the circulation, but do leave the firing line before doing this or you may distract other competitors. Your anatomical grip must not come so far back that it touches your wrist. In very cold or windy weather you may decide to wear a cover over the whole grip, but here again this must not give support to your wrist.

The free pistol grip should be so designed that the barrel is as low in the hand as possible, to reduce the turning moment between the line of the barrel and the centre of balance, which will be in the palm of your hand. This helps to reduce the amount of vertical movement at the muzzle when the shot breaks.

Because of the construction of the muscles and tendons in the hand and fingers, the amount of pressure exerted in the grip is directly related to the pressure which the index finger applies in operating the trigger. The lighter the trigger pressure, the less is the force exerted in the grip. As free pistols have very light triggers they must be held with minimal force so that the trigger finger may be uninhibited in its movement. Nevertheless, a firm hold is needed. To achieve this, the grip must fit the hand perfectly; thus the grip is an important factor in free pistol trigger control.

Trigger Control

We have already seen that if a conscious effort is made to release a shot when the aim appears to be correct, extra force will be used, which will

Free pistol grip: note how the wrist is bent downwards, so locking the wrist joint, and how the anatomical grip partially encloses the hand, while leaving the wrist free.

be in excess of that required to release the trigger normally. This will disturb the pistol and result in a poor shot.

The correct way to release a good shot is to apply a gradual build-up of pressure to the trigger, smoothly increasing to the amount required to release the shot, without anticipating the precise moment when the pistol will fire.

During the aiming process there will be a certain amount of sight movement which you should strive to control. The movement should gradually diminish until it ceases for a short time. After this short period of steadiness, the movement will increase again and become quite erratic. The release of the trigger should coincide with the period of least sight movement. No one can hold a pistol completely still, least of all a free pistol, but you should

endeavour to keep the movement within, say, the 9 ring. This amount of movement in the aim can be ignored, provided the sight picture is correct. Remember, parallel errors are acceptable, but angular errors *must* be avoided completely.

Free pistols have special triggers which can be adjusted to release at pressures as low as five grams. A light pressure has the advantage of allowing a shorter time to elapse between the eye recognising that the sight picture and aim are correct, and the release of the shot. But unless you can control this light pressure, it can work against you. All your movements must be slow and careful, as any sudden movement will disturb the sight alignment.

For normal temperatures you should set your trigger somewhere between 25 to 35 grams –

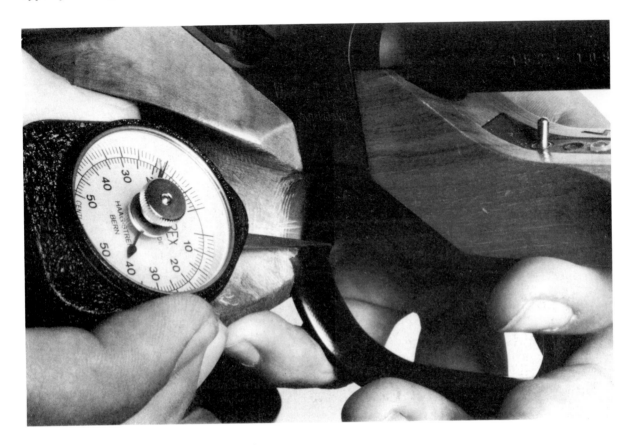

Measuring the trigger pressure of a free pistol using an accurate gauge.

perhaps heavier until you gain more experience. In cold weather, when your fingers lose their sensitivity, you may wish to increase this pressure, even up to as much as 150 grams. Provided you have practised with the trigger at this pressure, you should suffer no disadvantage.

Although the light trigger will enable you to release the shot very quickly, with little finger movement, you will spend proportionately more time in steadying your pistol, so the optimum time for shot release of 5 to 10 seconds, recommended in basic techniques, can be extended to 12 to 15 seconds in free pistol shooting.

AIR PISTOL

Course of Fire

The UIT air pistol match consists of 60 match shots fired in two and a quarter hours for men and junior men, and 40 match shots fired in one and a half hours for ladies and junior ladies. Both classes are shot at a distance of ten metres, using an air pistol with a calibre of 4.5mm (.177). The pistol with all its accessories fitted to it must not weigh more than 1,500 grams, and the trigger must lift a weight of 500 grams. Only one shot is fired at each target. An unlimited number of sighting shots may be fired before the start of the competition, and these are preceded by an unlimited number of warming-up shots fired at the pellet catcher.

Modification of Basic Technique

The basic slow-fire shooting technique must be modified to allow for the considerably slower muzzle velocity of the air pistol pellet.

Stance

This match lasts two and a quarter hours and your stance must therefore be free from strain to avoid fatigue. As you change your target after every shot, you will move about during the match, so you must be able to take up your stance easily and quickly each time you move. Moving about between shots will help your blood to return from your feet and legs, where it has a tendency to pool.

Grip

You will need to have well-shaped grips which exactly fit your hand because you will take up your grip for each shot. Changing targets with one hand is difficult and cocking air pistols by operating the cocking lever requires a fair

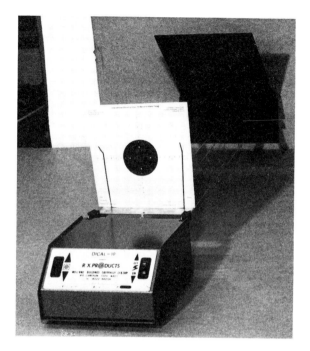

Air pistol target changer with pellet catcher and 10-metre target.

Preparing to take the grip on a Feinwerkbau CO₂ pistol.

amount of force, which may disturb your grip on the butt. Therefore you should make a habit of putting your pistol down after firing, and then setting yourself up afresh for each new shot.

Aiming

As the target is quite close and has a prominent aiming mark, there is a tendency for your eye to focus on it. To overcome this, and to keep your focus on the foresight, you should take a deep six o'clock area aim. It will help if you use a wide foresight, as your eye will be able to focus on a wide blade more easily than on a narrow one. The rearsight notch will need to be opened to accommodate the wider foresight picture.

Most air pistols come with an assortment of different sized foresight and rearsight elements. It will help you to focus on the foresight if it is well blackened with carbide soot.

Trigger Control

The time taken between the release of the trigger and the pellet leaving the barrel is much greater in an air pistol than in a normal pistol – as much as five times greater – and therefore any movement of the pistol while the pellet is in the barrel is going to have a marked effect on its trajectory. Correct trigger control is therefore vital. You must apply the pressure to the trigger more gently, in one long, even squeeze, to achieve a really smooth release. It is even more

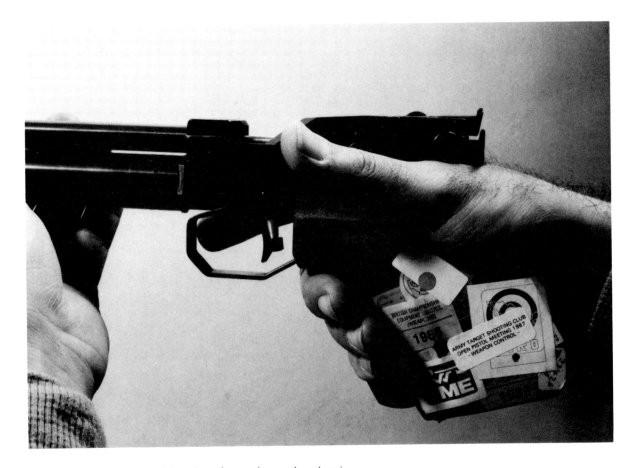

Wrapping the fingers around the grip and preparing to place the trigger finger in position on the trigger.

The final hold, with thumb relaxed and pressure applied in fore and aft axis. The pistol sits low in the hand, giving good control over trigger release and recoil.

The hold as seen from the right front quarter.

The correct hold: notice the position of the finger on the trigger.

important to squeeze the trigger directly to the rear; there must be no side pressure.

A common error with an air pistol is to apply a secondary pressure to the trigger. If, when you squeeze the trigger, you do not achieve its release, do not add more pressure; if you do, a snatch will result, which is even worse in an air pistol than in a normal pistol. Come down from your aiming position and start again, but this time apply more pressure from the beginning. Never alter the pressure while the pistol is on aim. Trigger release must be practised until you can release perfectly every time. Fortunately this is something which you can practise in your home.

The addition of barrel weights will help to reduce trigger release errors, as they help to damp out any small movements at the muzzle.

Of course they do add to the work you have to do in raising the pistol up into the aiming position, which will be many more times than the mere 60 shots plus sighters of the match. It is quite usual for a shooter to come on aim three times for every two shots fired.

Because correct trigger control is so vital to success with an air pistol, do practise shooting at a blank card from time to time during your training shoots, or even during your sighting series before a match. You will find that it will improve your control of the trigger immeasurably.

Follow-through

This is especially important in air pistol shooting because of the length of time between trigger release and the pellet leaving the barrel. We like Laslo Antal's analogy, comparing an air pistol pellet to a rocket which moves off a few seconds after ignition. Make sure your pellet has passed through the target before you start to come down off aim.

Training

Air pistol shooting is an absorbing discipline in its own right, but it is also a very useful training tool for other disciplines, particularly because you have to exercise fine trigger control and a well-developed follow-through. Another advantage is that you can set up an air pistol range in your home or garden; and pellets are cheaper than other ammunition.

There are several models of pellet catchers on sale which permit the target to be held in front of them. Alternatively you can invest in a proper automatic target changer. There are scaled-down ten-metre targets available for use at six yards, as well as the six-yard target itself. These are both useful for training at home.

Your training periods should be lengthened so that you regularly shoot far more than you would in any match. In this way you will build up your stamina, so that you shoot the full 60 shots plus sighters with ease.

Although air pistols do not emit harmful noises, it is a good idea to wear your ear-muffs or plugs to cut out extraneous noises from the range. This will help you to concentrate on releasing your shot.

RAPID-FIRE PISTOL

Course of Fire

The UIT Rapid-fire Pistol match consists of 60 competition shots divided into two courses of 30 shots each. Each course is subdivided into six series of five shots each; two in eight seconds, two in six seconds and two in four seconds. In each series, one shot is fired at each of five 25-metre rapid-fire pistol targets, at a distance of 25 metres.

Before the beginning of each course, you may shoot one sighting series of five shots in any of the time sequences you wish to nominate.

The pistol used in this event is a .22 made to fire a short cartridge, and the magazine holds five rounds. The pistol has to conform to certain limits: it must fit into a box measuring 300mm × 150mm × 50mm; and it must not weigh more than 1,260g. There is no restriction on the trigger weight, but as the pistol has to be held quite tightly, you are advised not to have too light a trigger.

Modification of Basic Technique

While it has been observed that rapid-fire shooting is only slow-fire shooting done quickly, this is an over-simplification. What it does mean is that the basic techniques of trigger control, sight picture maintenance and aim apply, but will need to be adapted. Your stance and breathing will need considerable modification and a new element will be introduced – the vertical raise.

Stance

Your stance must be slightly more braced than in slow-fire shooting, with your feet slightly further apart, to facilitate a quick and smooth vertical raise and the change of direction from one target to another. You should align yourself to engage the right-hand target first, and then shoot from right to left. In this way, if your last shot is delayed a fraction of a second, you make a small angle with the fifth target, and as the target turns it will still be facing you for a moment, increasing your chance of scoring. If you set up on any target other than the first – such as the middle target – you may be misaligned when coming up for the first shot. The necessary correction will take valuable time and have a detrimental psychological effect on the rest of the series. The change of aim from one target to the next *must* be made by pivoting at your hips, and on no account by movement of the arm alone as this will cause a misalignment of the sights. Imagine that your upper trunk is the gun turret on a tank, swivelling to

Walther rapid-fire pistol, showing the gas ports on top of the barrel and typical rapid-fire grip which partially encloses the hand.

engage different targets, while the body of the tank remains static.

Your feet should be at least as wide apart as your shoulders, a little more may be helpful, with your weight evenly distributed on each foot. A more oblique stance will help you to obtain a smooth vertical raise.

Vertical Raise

You start the rapid-fire match from what is known as the 'Ready' position. This is with the pistol held at an angle of 45 degrees from the vertical. To come up to the aiming position you could move your arm up as fast as possible – the fast rise – but if you did that you would almost certainly overshoot the aiming mark, and waste time while you brought your arm down to the correct aim. Alternatively, you could raise your arm deliberately – the slow rise – but this would take too long.

Therefore you should start your rise fast, and then slow down as the sights reach the bottom of

the target; at the same time, you start putting pressure on the trigger. You progressively slow your vertical movement until, as the sights reach the bottom of the ten zone, the trigger releases. With the vertically elongated scoring zones on this target, you have a certain latitude in the vertical aim – make use of it to enable you to obtain a clean let-off. You can accept small inaccuracies in aiming, provided your sight picture is correct, while you concentrate on timing. It will help if you have a fairly broad foresight, so that you can focus on it quickly, and a similarly broad rearsight notch which will give you a slightly wider gap either side of the foresight than you would use in other shooting.

During the vertical rise your head should be upright, in your firing stance; only your arm and your eyes should move. Your arm goes down to 45 degrees and your eyes try to focus a point in space about three feet (a metre) in front of you, whilst out of the upper edge of your eye you watch for the targets turning to face you.

Some coaches recommend that you alter the

speed of your vertical raise depending upon the time available in the series being shot. However, the differences for the eight, six and four-second series are so small that they are of mathematical interest only, and you are best advised to use the same speed throughout. If you can come up from the 'Ready' position and fire your first shot in one second, you will have sufficient time to fire the remaining four shots comfortably.

From the 'Ready' position you should watch the bottom of the targets out of the edge of your eye. As soon as they start to turn, you quickly and smoothly raise your pistol, whilst at the same time pushing it forward – imagine you have a leather tied on its end and are trying to wipe a curved glass window. Try to keep your focus on a point in space about three feet (a

metre) in front of you. Do not look at the targets fully, nor down at your sights. Wait for the sights to come up into your vision, then follow them up. As they pass the bottom of the target, start to decelerate your arm and start taking the pressure up on the trigger; and as the sights come into the bottom of the 10 zone, the shot should break.

As you are trying to release your first shot in one second, you have to do several things simultaneously:

1.   Make a smooth vertical raise through an arc of 45 degrees.
2.   Take up the pressure on the trigger.
3.   Ensure the sights are correctly aligned.
4.   See that the aim is within the tolerance allowed.

You can only do this if you practise these movements repeatedly to obtain perfect co-ordination and smoothness. This dry training can be done at home and should be done daily. When you come to shoot you will have no second chance; you have got to get it right the first, and every, time.

Trigger Control

In rapid-fire shooting opinion is divided on the type of trigger to be preferred. The roll-over type has the advantage that its smooth action does not disturb the sight picture. On the other hand, the breaking type of trigger allows some of the trigger pressure to be taken up during the vertical raise, and while the pistol is recovering from each successive let-off.

Apart from the first shot, the pistol must be stationary at the moment of let-off. Good scores are seldom made when shooting on the move. Bad shots are usually caused by faulty trigger control.

As part of the follow-through action, once the shot has been released you should move your trigger finger forward – still keeping it in touch with the trigger – ready for the next shot. If you fail to make a conscious effort to do this, sooner or later you are going to hold the trigger

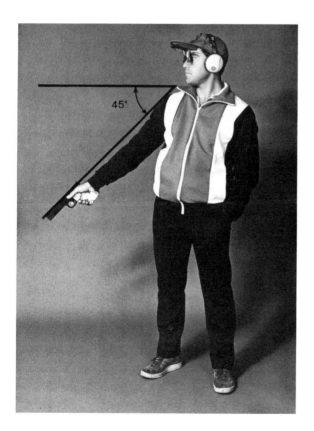

The 'Ready' position. The extended arm must be at least 45 degrees from the horizontal.

back from its previous release, resulting in a non-allowable malfunction.

Aiming

The psychological advantage gained from firing a well-aimed first shot will usually lead to good shots in the rest of the series. Conversely, any upset in the release of the first shot will be reflected in the other four. You will have to learn to accept inaccuracies in aiming due to the speed with which the shooting is carried out. Fortunately the size of the scoring zones permits a certain margin of error.

Opinion is divided on the precise point at which you should aim. Some people prefer to aim centrally, while others prefer a six o'clock aim. If you have no preference, we suggest you use a central aim.

As soon as the first shot has been released, you should start to pivot at the waist to align your sights with the second target. Keep the angle between your arm and your body constant. If you move your arm across to sight the next target, your sights will go out of alignment, and will also go increasingly lower. Stop when your sights reach the next ten zone and release the shot. Do not be tempted to fire when moving horizontally. Once again, as you turn, let your trigger finger go forward and start to take up the pressure for the next shot as the sights reach the centre of the target.

After you have fired the fifth shot, do not relax. Complete your recovery as with the previous shots and prepare to fire a sixth shot at an imaginary sixth target to the left of the fifth one. This is part of the follow-through action, and it helps to prevent you from losing your rhythm and momentum when firing the fifth shot. It thus helps to stop that one going low, as it might otherwise do.

Breathing

When you are ready to shoot, you will call 'Ready', and after a period of three seconds (plus or minus one second) the targets will turn to face you. Therefore, after you have called

'Ready', take a full breath, then slowly expel half of this whilst you wait for the targets to start turning. Then hold your breath until you have completed the series. With practice you can use your breathing rhythm to help you time the period, so that you know when to expect the targets to turn.

Maintenance

A rapid-fire shooter fires more rounds than people shooting other disciplines, so it is necessary to clean your pistol after every session to ensure it remains trouble-free. There really is no excuse for malfunctions due to lack of pistol maintenance.

SPORT PISTOL AND CENTRE-FIRE PISTOL

Course of Fire

Men shoot the Centre-fire Match, using centre-fire pistols, while ladies and juniors shoot the sport pistol event using small-bore standard pistols. In other respects the courses of fire are the same and consist of 60 shots divided into two stages of 30 shots each. The first stage is the precision stage, and the second stage is the rapid-fire stage (previously called the 'duelling' stage).

Precision Stage

This is shot at 25 metres at the international precision target. The 30 competition shots are fired in six series of five shots each, in a time of six minutes for each series. Before the beginning of the first competition series you may shoot a sighting series of five shots in six minutes.

Rapid-fire Stage

This is shot at 25 metres at the international rapid-fire target. The 30 competition shots are fired in six series of five shots each. During each series, the target is shown five times, each time for three seconds. The time between each appearance is seven seconds. Only one shot may be fired at each appearance. You must be in the 'Ready' position before the targets are turned to face you (that is, with gun and arm at an angle of 45 degrees from the vertical). After each shot you must return to the 'Ready' position. Before the first competition series you may fire a sighting series of five shots.

Modification of Basic Technique

Obviously there are two different techniques for the two very different stages.

Using a speed loader to re-load a 6 chamber revolver.

An in-line stance, here being demonstrated for use in the centre-fire event using a .32 Britarms Mk 3.

Precision Stage

This is a straightforward slow-fire shoot in which the basic techniques are applied. To succeed in this match you must obtain very good scores in the precision stage, and you must therefore apply those techniques of stance, grip, trigger control, sight picture, aiming and breath control which were mentioned in Chapter 2. Make full use of the time allowed.

Duelling Stage

This is rather similar to firing the first shot in the rapid-fire pistol match thirty times, so you must master your fast/slow vertical raise. You should commence the vertical raise rapidly and smoothly and as the sights pass the bottom of the target you should decrease the speed of raise smoothly, so that the pistol stops in the aiming area without overshooting it.

When you set yourself up, practise the fast/slow vertical raise so that your stance, relative to the target, is correct and the sights come up along the vertical axis passing through the target's centre. Repeat this procedure several times to ensure your stance is correct.

As you have three seconds in which to raise your pistol from the 'Ready' position and fire, you should use as much of this time as possible to fire a deliberate shot. Try practising to release your shot in 2.8 seconds.

After each appearance of the target it will turn away for a period of seven seconds. This is insufficient time for you to alter your grip, and so you must be very sure you have the right grip at the beginning of each series. This seven seconds waiting time must be mastered, as it means that you must maintain a tight grip on your pistol for something like 46 seconds during each five-shot series. This is a long time, and you must train in order to have the strength to be able to keep your grip constant throughout this period.

If you use a revolver for this match, cock the trigger with your other hand and release each shot from the fully cocked position. This will prevent any risk of disturbing your grip.

Your breathing rhythm is important in this match. As the targets turn away, take a good full breath. As they turn to face you, and you start your vertical raise, exhale half of this breath, and then hold your breath until after you have released your shot. As you lower your pistol to the 'Ready' position take another full breath, and so on. In this way you will keep your blood oxygenated and your breathing rhythm will help you to 'count' the seven seconds between exposures of the target.

STANDARD PISTOL

Course of Fire

The Standard Pistol event consists of 60 competition shots divided into three stages of 20 shots each, all shot at 25 metres at the international precision target. Each stage consists of four series of five shots. Before the competition begins you are allowed a sighting series of five shots in 150 seconds.

The first stage is a slow-fire stage consisting of four series of five shots, each fired in 150 seconds. The second stage is a timed-fire stage consisting of four series of five shots, each fired in 20 seconds. The third stage is a rapid-fire stage consisting of four series of five shots, each fired in ten seconds.

Modification of Basic Technique

One of the attractions of this event is that it is really three separate courses of fire: slow or precision; timed fire and rapid fire. Each course requires different techniques.

Precision Stage

Firing five shots in 150 seconds requires the application of all the basic pistol shooting techniques, with perhaps the one exception that we do not recommend you plot each shot after it has been fired. There is insufficient time to do this without losing your concentration and rhythm.

As the aiming mark on this target is rather large and is relatively close, you may find your eye is drawn towards it. Therefore you will need to pay even more attention to keeping your focus on your foresight. Things which will help you to do this are taking a deeper six o'clock aim, having well blackened sights and using a fairly broad foresight blade with a correspondingly wide rearsight notch.

Timed and Rapid-fire Stages

To succeed in these stages you will need to modify your basic technique in several areas:

1. *The vertical raise*: as you must be in the 'Ready' position before the commencement of each series, you will need to practise bringing your pistol up to the aiming position smoothly and quickly. Although in 20 seconds you would have time to use a slow raise, there seems little point in not keeping to one speed for all your requirements, and you should therefore use the fast/slow raise method. In the ten second series

you will certainly need to use the fast/slow raise.

Whenever you use the vertical raise in your shooting, you must ensure you have the right stance, compatible with the speed of raise you are using. To find your correct stance you must practise the vertical raise several times, always at the same speed that you will use in the match. If your sights are not coming up exactly through the centre of the target, move your feet to bring the pistol on to the correct line.

2.   *Grip*: as you will have to control the recoil of five successive shots, you must take a firmer grip than in slow-fire shooting. To avoid fatigue affecting your grip towards the end of the stage, you should do regular arm and hand strengthening exercises.

3.   *Trigger control*: when you shoot timed-fire events you must be careful that the quick trigger release you want does not become a snatch. You must practise your trigger release daily (dry training) to master the fast, but smooth, release which is so necessary.

You will have to practise taking up the initial trigger pressure for the release of the second shot whilst recovering from the first recoil. This you can practise by firing shots in pairs.

4.   *Sight picture and aiming*: because of the restricted time available, you cannot afford to spend too long in achieving the perfect aim, but neither can you risk snatching a haphazard shot. Therefore you have to learn a new technique – that of releasing a shot when the aim is less than perfect. Provided the sight picture is correct you can accept a small area of tolerance around the perfect aim.

5.   *Shot release timing*: if you hang on to your first and last shots in a series to try to make them good ones, you will become too anxious about those shots, and/or about the timing of the whole series, with the result that you may well snatch those shots and achieve a poor score. You must built up a well-defined rhythm. Some shooters think that 'rhythm' is a series of equally spaced bangs. That is 'cadence', the end product of rhythm, and if heard by the shooter, it shows that all your concentration is not being kept on the matters in hand (and mind) – sight picture and trigger squeeze. You

should 'hear' the recoil but not the sound.

There are various shot release timings which can be used. For instance, some shooters prefer to fire their shots in pairs by starting the next release whilst recovering from the previous shot; that is, shooting on the follow-through. However, it is preferable to make each release a deliberately aimed shot, using the timings below.

20-second stage:
1st shot 3 seconds
2nd shot 4 seconds, elapsed time 7 seconds
3rd shot 4 seconds, elapsed time 11 seconds
4th shot 4 seconds, elapsed time 15 seconds
5th shot 4 seconds, elapsed time 19 seconds
Safety
margin   1 second, elapsed time 20 seconds

10-second stage:
1st shot 2 seconds
2nd shot 1.8 seconds, elapsed time 3.8 seconds
3rd shot 1.8 seconds, elapsed time 5.6 seconds
4th shot 1.8 seconds, elapsed time 7.4 seconds
5th shot 1.8 seconds, elapsed time 9.2 seconds
Safety
margin   0.8 seconds, elapsed time 10 seconds

There are several other forms of competitive shooting.

ADVANCING MEN

Course of Fire

There are separate competitions for centre-fire pistol and small-bore pistol, but the rules are the same. You are faced with three Figure 11 (59) targets, and two shots have to be fired at each one. You may hold your pistol with one or two hands, but must be in the 'Ready' position at the start. The targets start at 25 yards and advance to ten yards in a period of eight seconds. They are mounted on a trolley which runs along rails, and when the trolley reaches the ten-yard point a trip turns the targets edge on, so any late shot will not hit the face of the target.

Modification of Basic Technique

Apart from the fact that you may hold your pistol in two hands, the main modification of the basic technique is one of timing. This exciting competition is a battle of nerves. If you start to shoot quickly, the targets are well away from you and any error will lose you points. The recommended technique is to raise your pistol in the usual fast/slow raise, check your sight picture and then pause while the targets approach. If you have taken two seconds for your raise and a further one second to check your sight picture and aim, you will have five seconds in which to fire the six shots. After three seconds the targets will be about 20 yards away, so you should fire two well-aimed shots at the right-hand target. Now swing to engage the middle target where you will fire rather more

quickly, with the fact that the targets are now nearer compensating for any error in aiming. Then swing to engage the third target, which by now will be some 12 yards away and will look very close. You will have approximately two seconds in which to fire the last two shots. This will mean firing the sixth shot on the recovery from the recoil of the fifth shot.

Although the rules permit holding the pistol in two hands, the conventional single-handed hold is preferable, as this puts the sights further from your eye and provides a better sight picture which can be more easily focused.

As with all rapid-fire events, you will need to take a firmer grip than you would use for slow-fire shooting.

Note that this competition requires you to fire six shots. This is fine for a revolver, but when using many types of semi-automatic pistol

Advancing Men being shot at Bisley.

you will need to load the first round into the breech, after cocking your pistol, and then carefully insert the magazine with the other five rounds.

AMERICAN 2700

Course of Fire

The National Match Course consists of a series of shooting for an aggregate of 900 points, using a .22 calibre pistol. The whole series is then shot again using any centre-fire pistol for an aggregate of 1,800 points. It is re-shot using a .45 calibre pistol to reach the 2,700 points maximum. You will see that you do not have to use three different pistols to shoot this course, as the .45 could be used to shoot the centre-fire series. This event calls for the mastery of different weapons and as such is an interesting event in which to compete.

The actual details of the course are:

1. 20 shots, slow fire, at 50 yards, at the B – 6 target, in four strings of five shots, each fired in five minutes.
2. 20 shots, timed fire, at 25 yards, at the B – 8 target, in four strings of five shots, each fired in 20 seconds.
3. 20 shots, rapid fire, at 25 yards, at the B – 8 target, in four strings of five shots, each fired in ten seconds.
4. A repeat of the first three elements, but firing ten shots each time, that is, 30 shots in all.

Modification of Basic Technique

You will notice the similarity between this event and the standard pistol UIT event. However, there are three important differences. The first is that this is a longer competition and requires considerable stamina, which must be built up by specialised training. The second difference concerns the use of the centre-fire pistol for this type of event, and the third is that you may be on aim at the start of the timed and rapid-fire series, which gives a considerable advantage.

Stamina Training

Under normal circumstances, you will probably be in the habit of firing no more than 100 shots in any shooting session. To fire 270 shots, two-thirds with centre-fire pistols, means that you must train your whole body to meet these conditions, so you will intensify your physical training programme. In particular you will need to strengthen your grip. This can be achieved by including more finger and wrist strengthening exercises, such as the use of a spring apparatus to strengthen your fingers, and press-ups done from the fingertips instead of with the palm of the hand on the floor. This additional strength cannot be created overnight; it must be built up gradually over a period of some three months.

Shot Timing

In the slow-fire series the basic techniques apply without modification; but in the timed and rapid-fire series the advice given for dealing with the UIT standard pistol event also applies here (*see* page 89). As the rules permit you to be on aim at the start of each series, you will not have to practise the vertical raise, but instead you should practise taking up the first pressure of your trigger release and holding it. Then, as soon as the series begins, you will be on aim and ready to release your first shot, giving more time to fire the remaining four shots deliberately. This is a particular advantage when shooting a .45 in the rapid-fire series.

BARGRAVE DEAN

This is a team event, best shot with centre-fire pistols. When shot in the NRA Imperial meeting, the team consists of three people.

Course of Fire

In this event each person loads his pistol with six rounds and this is placed, uncocked, on a bench 15 yards from the targets. Each team has 15 clay

The Bargrave Dean: a Parachute Regiment team shooting in the Regular Army Meeting at Bisley.

discs (clay pigeons painted white) as targets, and these are fastened to sticks about six inches above the ground. The teams withdraw 50 yards from the bench. When the competition starts, the teams have 30 seconds in which to run the 50 yards, pick up and cock their pistols, and shoot at the targets.

The winners are the team who break all the discs first, or who break the most discs. If each team has broken the same number of targets, then the team which has used the least ammunition will win.

Modification of Basic Technique

The way to succeed in this event is to keep calm and not let the excitement of the occasion overcome your basic shooting skill. When running forward, do not over-exert yourself. There are no prizes for being first to start firing, only for breaking the targets!

Have a plan so that each member of the team knows at which targets he will aim. Ideally the two end persons should start at their respective ends and work towards the middle; while the

The Bargrave Dean: scoring the hits.

Scene during the British Pistol Championships on Century range.
Shooting one of the team events.

middle person should aim first at target number six and work to the right.

CONVENTIONAL AND CLUB COMPETITIONS

Course of Fire

There are various types of competition in this category, but they have one element in common, which is that they are basically slow-fire events requiring ten shots to be fired in ten minutes. The distance may be 20 yards, 25 yards, 25 metres, 50 yards or 50 metres.

Sometimes the rules permit the use of a free pistol, compensating for any unfair advantage

It is unusual for a highest possible score to be shot in the Mayleigh postal international match. Here Paul Leatherdale is seen with the 100 he scored in 1987. The NRA of America target has a prominent 'X' ring in the middle of the ten ring. Paul scored four 'tens' and six 'X's. The target was autographed by his fellow team members and officials.

this might bring with a declared average at the start of the competition which puts the competitors into the correct class. Otherwise the pistol will usually be either a small-bore, which will have to lift a trigger weight of 1kg in Europe or 2lb in the United States or a centre-fire pistol which will lift a trigger weight of 1,360g in Europe or 4lb in the United States.

Modification of Basic Technique

In this type of slow-fire shooting, all the advice in Chapter 2 on basic techniques applies without modification. The only variation is in the grip to be used in holding a centre-fire pistol.

Centre-fire Pistol Grip

Quite apart from the need to hold the grip of a centre-fire pistol more firmly than that of a small-bore pistol, to control the recoil, many people prefer to use revolvers for this type of shooting. The shape of a revolver butt differs from that of a semi-automatic pistol, and requires a slightly different hold. The little finger should exert some pressure to assist in the grip, whereas it should take very little part in holding a semi-automatic pistol. The thumb, too, has a new role. Most revolvers have two methods by which the hammer may be cocked. Many, but not all, have a spur at the back of the hammer by which it may be drawn back into the cocked position. In these pistols you have the choice of using the thumb of your shooting hand to press on the spur to cock the pistol, or you may use your other hand to cock it in this way. But you also have the option of cocking the pistol by drawing back the trigger (known as 'pulling through') where the pistol has a double action, as indeed you have to do in revolvers which have no hammer spur. Using the thumb of your shooting hand to cock the hammer will inevitably disturb your grip and is not recommended. You would be well advised to practise pulling through on the double action because once you have perfected this method you can shoot without disturbing your grip or

Shooting the Ladies Pistol Championships at Bisley, 1985.

stance. If you choose to cock the revolver using your non-shooting hand, you will have to remove it from its resting place and bring it across your body to reach the pistol, while at the same time bending your shooting elbow to bring the pistol closer to you. This can upset your perfect stance.

Due to the construction of the muscles, tendons and nerves in the hand, the pressure on the trigger and the pressure exerted in holding the grip are interrelated. Inevitably the pressure needed to release a trigger which will lift a weight of 1,360g will dictate that your hold on the butt will be firmer, which you would want it to be anyway, to control the heavier recoil and speed your recovery after each shot. If you are pulling through, you will be applying even more pressure to the trigger.

DISC BREAKING

You can make up your own rules for disc breaking competitions. The Bargrave Dean is a suitable one for centre-fire pistols. However, for small-bore pistols you need to use two-inch white clay discs fixed against a black background.

Course of Fire

The NSRA competition involves teams of two or three, using standard small-bore pistols firing .22 long rifle ammunition. There is an unlimited number of rounds per person and the time allowed is one minute. The first team to break all their discs or the team to break the most discs is the winner. If the teams are equal, there is a re-shoot.

95

Long-range pistol shooting: note the supported hold – only the butt may rest on a support – the telescopic sight, and shooter's back support.

Modification of Basic Technique

It is very difficult in the excitement of this type of competition to take an area aim successfully, so you should adjust your sights to take a centre aim – bearing in mind that you have black sights against a white target. Keep calm and fire well-aimed, well-released shots, paying particular attention to your trigger control. It is so easy to snatch the trigger in the heat of the moment.

As in the Bargrave Dean competition, have a plan so that each team member knows which disc to aim at, to prevent the whole team firing at the same disc at the beginning.

LONG-RANGE PISTOL

Long-range pistol shooting is a very specialised discipline which has almost as much to do with rifle shooting as it does with pistol shooting. Although the International Long Range Pistol Association was not formed until 1975, military pistols have been used to shoot at ranges up to 500 metres for very many years, but usually only by the addition of a stock to the back of the butt to turn them into carbines. Examples are the 9mm and 7.6mm Mausers, the 9mm Luger semi-automatic pistols, and some Webley revolvers.

Course of Fire

There are several different competitions available for the long-range pistol shooter. In all of them the pistol may be held in one or two hands, provided that neither hand holds the pistol forward of the trigger guard. Any stance may be adopted, the more usual ones being standing in a slit trench, sitting against some form of back support, or lying prone. If you choose to stand in a trench you are permitted to rest your hand or hands on a sandbag. The principle courses of fire available are:

1. *Service pistol*: this is for service pistols as defined in the NRA rules, and consists of two sighters and ten shots to count at 100 and 200 yards. At 100 yards the target used is the Wessex which has vertically elongated scoring zones; and at 200 yards the target is the British Army four-foot rifle target.

2. *Pocket pistol*: this is for pistols whose barrel length does not exceed three and a half inches. It is only shot at 100 yards, using the Wessex target.

3. *All-comers*: in this competition any centre-fire pistol may be used whose rifled barrel length does not exceed nine inches, whose sight base does not exceed 12 inches, and whose trigger weight is a minimum of three pounds.

Shooting is two sighters and ten shots to count at 100, 200 and 300 yards, giving an

Long-range pistol shooting at 300 yards. The pistol is a 7.62mm Kengil made by Modern & Antique Firearms of Bournemouth, and has a 12-inch barrel.

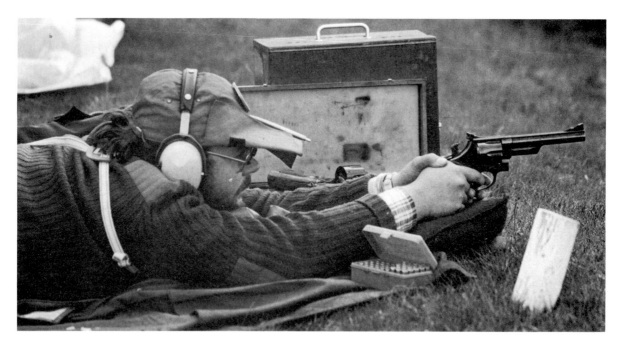

Long-range pistol, prone position.

Long-range pistol shooting at 300 yards.

Long-range black powder shooting at Bisley on a rainy day.

aggregate score of 150 points. At 100 yards the Wessex target is used, while at 200 and 300 yards the British Army four-foot and 500 targets are used respectively.

4.   *Colt .45*: this is open to users of the Colt .45 government pistol, or any copy of its design. Shooting is at 100 yards at the Wessex target and at 200 yards at the British Army four-foot rifle target. Once again, the shoot consists of two sighters and ten shots to count at each range.

5.   *Free pistol*: as the title suggests, any centre-fire pistol may be used, provided that the rifled barrel length does not exceed nine and a half inches. Telescopic sights are permitted in this event. Shooting is at the British Army four-foot rifle target at 200 yards and at the British Army 500 target at 300 yards. At each range two sighters and ten shots to count are fired.

6.   *Black powder*: this is open only to percussion pistols having a maximum barrel length of ten inches, and is shot at 100 yards at the Wessex target. The shoot consists of two sighters and ten shots to count.

Modification of Basic Technique

Obviously several modifications of the basic techniques are needed when you come to shoot long-range pistol events. While the correct grip, good trigger control, correct breathing and an accurate sight picture are still vitally important, you will need to acquire new skills from the field of rifle shooting, such as judging wind strength and direction, studying light effect and mirage, and paying attention to the type of ammunition you use. Factory-loaded ammunition is not usually suitable for these weapons and ranges, and you will need to learn about home loading, which is a specialised subject in its own right.

Muzzle loaders shooting their black powder charges on the Gallery Range at Bisley.

Black powder shooting with a Colt 36 at Bisley.

Shooting the police pistol competition. At top left there is an ejected case from the first shooter on the left's pistol on which the slide has already closed ready for the next shot. The fifth shooter from the left's slide is right back and the fired case is just emerging from the pistol.

Sight Picture

With the relatively short sight base and long range, any angular error is heavily punished, so you must exercise great care to maintain the correct sight picture.

Trigger Control

As with the sight picture you need to be very careful not to disturb the pistol while squeezing the trigger.

MUZZLE-LOADING PISTOL

Course of Fire

There are two types of competition for muzzle-loading pistols, depending upon whether the pistol is an original make or a reproduction. The course of fire is the same, being 13 shots in thirty minutes with the best ten shots to count. An unusual feature of muzzle-loading scoring is that if a shot breaks a scoring line the value of the hit is given according to the zone in which the majority of the hole lies. The target is the UIT 25-metre precision target.

A score of 99 in the same police pistol series.

Modification of Basic Technique

First of all, a two-handed hold is permitted and some shooters use their non-shooting hand to brace their other wrist, helping to control the quite considerable recoil. Muzzle-loading pistols use a propellant of black powder which burns more slowly than modern explosives, resulting in a slower and larger recoil, which lasts longer. For this reason it is necessary to control the recoil peoperly, and a well-developed follow-through must be used.

POLICE PISTOL

Course of Fire

This consists of 26 shots divided into three 'practices' and is shot using any centre-fire pistol with a calibre of .354 to .455. The targets are the international rapid-fire targets or the PAA (Police Athletic Association) figure targets if the Mander version is being shot.

Practice I: ten shots in five minutes at 25 metres.
Practice II: ten shots in two strings of five at 15 yards; the targets make five appearances of two seconds each, with an interval of five seconds between appearances. Two shots only are fired at each appearance.

Practical Pistol *(a)*   *Placing the loaded pistol in the holster.*

Practice III: six shots at ten metres. The targets make three appearances of two seconds each with an interval of five seconds between appearances. Two shots are fired at each appearance.

The pistol may be held with both hands. In Practices II and III the shooter must be in the 'Ready' position before each appearance.

Modification of Basic Technique

The modifications of basic technique concern grip and timing. In common with other centre-fire shooting, and where several shots have to be fired in quick succession, you must take a very firm and positive grip before the competition begins. There is not time to alter your grip in Practices II and III.

Those using revolvers should cock their pistols before each shot in Practice I and should cock by pulling through in Practices II and III if holding the pistol with one hand. If you choose to hold the pistol with two hands, and have a cocking spur on your hammer, then by all means cock your pistol using your non-shooting hand.

To raise your pistol from the 'Ready' position and fire two shots in two seconds in Practice III requires you to shoot the second shot as you recover from the recoil of the first shot, that is, to shoot on the follow-through. This is a technique which you need to practise and this is easily done by practising firing shots in pairs.

Practical Pistol *(b)* *Ready.*

PRACTICAL PISTOL

Unlike other forms of competitive pistol shooting, there are few formal rules for Practical Pistol competition because each event tries to put the shooter in a realistic, unusual situation. The general rules covering all events will be explained at the start of each competition, after the rules applying to safety, which are just as strict as in all other types of shooting. Points are normally scored for speed and accuracy, and for hitting power, in as much as a hit with a heavily loaded bullet will gain more marks than a similar hit with one of lighter load or calibre.

There are certain features which occur in most competitions: shooting with your strong hand; shooting with your weak hand; shooting with both hands; reloading quickly after shooting one series and before moving to the next position; firing on the move; and shooting at 'opportunity' targets which appear unexpectedly,

whilst avoiding 'no shoot' targets (such as a hostage being held in front of a criminal). Whilst the targets do simulate real situations, they are, of course, only paper targets, and practical pistol is just a sport.

Modification of Basic Technique

As might be expected there are many and various modifications to the basic techniques recommended in Chapter 2, but they are still only modifications of those techniques. They do not alter the basic elements. If you want to succeed, you must still carry out all the procedures correctly.

Grip

As you will have to use each hand singly and together at various times, you will need to practise holding your pistol in these situations. You are still endeavouring to maintain a firm

Practical Pistol *(c)* *Aiming.*

Practical Pistol *(d)* *Follow-through and recovery. Notice the ejected case above the shooter's head and the two-handed grip being used.*

grip which will allow you to control the recoil, perhaps while you prepare to fire the next shot on the follow-through from the first. Whether you are standing, kneeling, sitting, prone, or rolling over, nothing changes the basic requirement to maintain a firm grip which allows you to control your pistol. Dry training in exercising the various forms of grip will enable you to improve your grip control.

The recommended two-handed hold is to grip your pistol with your primary shooting hand in the normal manner, ensuring that the barrel is in line with your forearm, then wrap your secondary hand around your other hand, keeping its index finger below the trigger guard.

Sighting

As speed is usually of paramount importance, you need to be able to pick up your sight picture quickly, even in poor light. Therefore you may find you will need a wider foresight and a correspondingly wider rearsight notch.

Sometimes you may be using a short-barrelled pistol, which will mean that you will have a shorter sight base than might otherwise be the case. In this situation you must be very careful that you have the correct sight picture, as an angular error will put your bullet wide of its mark, even at short range.

Trigger Control

The fact that you need to release your shot quickly makes good trigger control even more

A Norwegian shooter shows the two-handed grip in Practical Pistol.

The kneeling position in the Practical Pistol event.

important than in slower disciplines. A snatched shot is no answer to the need for speed. Use dry training to learn the feel of your trigger, to know how to take up and hold the first pressure of your trigger with either hand, and how to achieve its smooth release.

Stance

Variations in stance will be dictated by the circumstances of the competition, but there is still the need to provide as stable a platform for your gun hand as possible. Keep your feet well apart, and your body over the triangle subtended by them.

Breathing

When you are firing after moving with some exertion, you will need to breathe deeply as you prepare to fire. This will help to stop your ribcage moving as the body tries to fulfil its need for more oxygen. If there is time for two deep

Practical Pistol (a) *Drawing from the holster while being timed by the umpire.*

breaths, so much the better. After firing, breathe deeply while you are reloading. With so much else to think about, you may forget this helpful activity if you do not make a conscious effort to gain oxygen and to control your pulse-rate.

Equipment

In some ways the equipment you need to shoot Practical Pistol is simpler than for other disciplines. For example, you will not need a telescope. Provided you have a suitable pistol, ear protectors, and shooting glasses, the other equipment you will need is particular to Practical Pistol shooting. A holster for your pistol is the first requirement, and there is a wide range from which to choose. Make sure that it is suitable for your pistol, and that you can effect a quick draw from it. It should be capable of retaining your pistol even if you are upside-down. You will also need spare magazines; some are elongated to take more than the usual number of cartridges allowed after the first load. If you use a revolver you will need speed loaders which hold the cartridges correctly spaced, ready to reload the cylinder in one

action. You will also need pouches to hold your speed loader or loaders, and any spare magazines for your semi-automatic pistol, on your belt.

Practical Pistol *(b)   Firing from behind cover.*

Practical Pistol *(c)   One way of shooting in the prone position.*

'The Falling Man'   *In this 'fun' shoot, the target falls backwards when a hit is registered in its centre area. It can be shot against another competitor or against the clock.*

SERVICE PISTOL

Course of Fire

This consists of 24 shots fired at the Figure 11 (59) target, the shots being divided into four practices.

Practice I: six shots in 15 seconds at 25 yards.
Practice II: six shots in ten seconds at 20 yards, three shots being fired at each of two targets.
Practice III: six shots at 15 yards. The targets make three appearances of three seconds each, with irregular intervals between them varying between three and ten seconds. Two shots only are fired at each appearance. Pistols must be returned to the 'Ready' position before each appearance.
Practice IV: six shots in six seconds at ten yards, three shots being fired at each of two targets.

Modification of Basic Technique

Much the same modifications as were recommended for the police pistol event apply to the service pistol event, the one difference being in Practice III. Here a new element enters the scene, with the irregular interval between target appearances. This calls for a quicker reaction than usual to the targets beginning to turn to face you. As in the UIT rapid-fire event you need to have your eyes focused about three feet (a metre) in front of you, watching out of the edge of your eye for the targets beginning to turn, and then picking up and focusing on your sights as the pistol comes up into your cone of vision.

4 Training

Unless you have a plan formulated to organise your training, it is likely that you will fail to accomplish all that you should. Training divides into two types: your long-term or strategic training and your short-term or tactical training. Both should be accommodated by your overall training plan.

So many factors combine in firing a successful shot that to think of all of them at the right time requires your full concentration. Your training programme will help to make some of those factors subconscious actions so that more of your conscious efforts can be devoted to the other factors.

TRAINING PLAN

To make your plan, start with the date of your final objective, which may be to be in top condition for an annual national pistol meeting, for example. The date of this event sets your datum, and now you go back in time some four months. This will be the start of your strategic plan. Set yourself the daily and/or weekly activity you decide is necessary to improve your physical condition and technical proficiency by the desired amount, and enter this on the chart. For instance, you may decide that you will run or jog for 15 minutes every day, and swim for 30 minutes twice a week. In your tactical training you may decide that you will do dry training on trigger control for 15 minutes, three times a week, so enter that. In this way you build up your plan to guide your training.

Having a well thought out plan will not make you fit; you also need the dedication and will-power to keep to your plan. You must put some effort into your exercises – it is not sufficient just to go through the motions. One of the differences between an average shooter and a potential champion is that the latter is more dedicated to the sport. He will put the maximum effort into training, even when pressures of business, social or family commitments make it difficult. If a day's activity has to be lost, the dedicated shooter will do twice as much the next day. Such a pattern is not necessarily to be commended, but it is better than missing your training altogether. It is best to do a little training often and regularly, rather than doing a lot occasionally.

PHYSICAL TRAINING

You do not need bulging muscles to be a successful pistol shooter, but you do need to have supple muscles of reasonable strength, and you certainly need your lungs and heart to be in prime condition.

Strategic Training

Your long-term physical training should be designed to build up your general fitness step by step, and then maintain it at the chosen level. It will include such activities as swimming, running, jogging, skipping, running on the spot and aerobic exercises. All these activities will help to get your muscles into good shape, but more importantly they will develop your heart and lungs. It is very important that these are well developed in a pistol shooter for, as we have already seen, you need to hold your breath whilst on aim and yet you also need a plentiful supply of fully oxygenated blood. Doctor Antal makes the point in his book *Competitive Pistol Shooting*, where he shows that, when resting, the pulse-rate of an untrained person might be 80 beats per minute, compared with 55 beats for a trained person whose heart circulates the same amount of blood with fewer pumps. During competition the pulse-rate will rise by 50 per cent. For the untrained person this will bring it up to 120 beats per minutes, seriously interfering with the ability to hold a pistol steady. For the trained person the rate will be increased to 80 beats per minute – the resting pulse of the untrained person. Think about that for a moment.

Your strategic training should be planned to improve your general fitness by steps. Do not attempt to make a large improvement too quickly – it could be dangerous and the benefits, such as they might be, could be short-lived. What you want is to make steady progress over a period of three to four months and, when you have reached your goal, to maintain that standard by carrying out a reduced training plan, still based on the principle of little and often.

Diet is part of your strategic training. Eating a properly designed, balanced diet plays a large part in maintaining a fit body, so make sure you are eating enough of the right food, and are not eating harmful substances. Avoid butter, animal fats, coffee and tea in large quantities.

Having got the food into your body, do not neglect getting rid of the waste products. Part of your strategic plan should be to train your body to function regularly at a time convenient to your shooting, such as first thing in the morning. In this way you will arrive on the firing line comfortable in your bowels and bladder, and benefiting from having got rid of waste gases, acids and other un-helpful material.

Tactical Training

This part of your training plan will involve those parts of the body particularly concerned with holding a pistol steady and firing a shot. Initially you will place more emphasis on your strategic training, but as your level of fitness rises and the datum date gets nearer, you will need to increase the amount of tactical training you do.

These exercises are intended to strengthen your shoulder, arm, wrist and finger muscles, to loosen your neck, and to keep your eye muscles supple and elastic. Like your strategic plan, your tactical plan should be constructed to build up the strength of the muscles concerned in steps.

1. *Arms, wrists and fingers*: hold your pistol on aim for periods of time which you gradually increase from 30 seconds to a minute, keeping the sights within a small circle marked on a card which you can place on the opposite wall. You should adopt a normal shooting stance, and hold your breath just as you would in real shooting.

Hold the chair as if it was a pistol, using second and third fingers, and sight a corner on an object across the room. Increase the length of time you hold it on aim, and the frequency of the exercise as your muscles strengthen.

(a)   To strengthen and loosen your arm and shoulder muscles, make large circles with your arms. Put some effort into your movement, making the circles as large as possible.

This exercise can be augmented by one which will speed up some of its benefits. If you fit weights to your wrist you can increase the amount of work your arm and wrist muscles have to do. Alternatively, you can achieve some of the benefits from this type of exercise by using a kitchen chair. Ideally use a chair which has square legs. In any event, do not wrap your fingers around the chair leg, but try to hold it as you would a pistol, with your index finger and thumb taking no part in the hold at all. Lift the chair up and sight some part of it against an object across the room, such as a light switch. Once again, assume your normal shooting stance as closely as possible, holding your breath at times, although at other times you

may breathe normally. Try to hold the chair on aim, keeping it as still as possible. Do not choose a chair which is too heavy or you may strain a muscle. Initially hold the chair up for a few seconds at a time, and then put it down in such a way that your muscles are completely relaxed. Then pick it up again and repeat the exercise. Each day try to hold the chair on aim for a longer period at a time, and increase the number of times you repeat the exercise.

When you become bored with simply holding the chair up on aim, there are small variations you can make which will also help your muscles. From the aiming position move the chair horizontally, trying to keep it as steady as possible while you move your arm from left to

(b)   Feel your muscles being exercised. Start with two minutes a day and increase the duration as you gain strength.

(a) Increasing chest expansion, so benefiting your breathing. Start with hands meeting in front of your chest, palms downwards.

(b) Beat backwards, quickly.

(c) Push as far back as you can, then come back to the starting position and repeat.

right and back again, perhaps following the horizontal line of a window frame.

Once you are on aim, you can close your eyes and count the lapse of, say, ten seconds, then open your eyes and see how far the chair has moved off aim. In all these exercises you can time yourself by counting off the seconds mentally using the words 'one hundred and one ... one hundred and two ...' and so on for each second. Occasionally check your counting against a stop-watch or the second hand of a clock to maintain a degree of accuracy.

A useful arm-rotating exercise is to stand with your feet slightly apart, keeping your arms straight and bringing them up above your head, then circling them backwards, down and up in front of you. Try to make the circle they trace as large as possible, and put some effort into it. Do this for two minutes to start with, and gradually increase the time each day until you are doing it

for five minutes each time.

Follow the arm-rotating exercise by bringing your arms up so that your fingertips just meet each other across your chest, with the palms facing downwards. Keeping your arms level, open your arms out and beat backwards, then bring them back across your chest. Again, repeat this exercise for a minute at the beginning, but gradually increase it to five minutes a day.

A good exercise to strengthen your wrists is to hold your arms forward with your elbows at your sides, with your palms uppermost and hands closed make your hands circle as large a circle as possible, keeping your forearms still. A variation of this will help to alleviate 'tennis elbow'. Whilst doing the same exercise push your hands forward until the arms are straight, and then bring your elbows back to your sides and so on.

112

(a)   Strengthen your wrists by rotating them in as large a circle as possible. Keep your elbows in at your sides.

(b)   A variation to follow your wrist-rotating exercise is to do the same but then move your arms forward as you rotate the wrists and push forwards.

Dumb-bells, or other weights, can be used to benefit arm and body muscles, here seen being used to strengthen arms and shoulders.

There are several exercises you can do with weights or dumb-bells which will strengthen your arms, wrists and fingers, but make sure you do not do too much, too soon and so strain a muscle. Using weights, however, makes use of a static force whereas in shooting you want elasticity. This can be achieved by using an elastic rope, or a section cut from an inner tube, to act as a spring to pull against your arm. Fit this to some elastic cord to extend it to the length of the gap from the floor to your hand when in the 'Ready' position. Put your foot in one end and your wrist at the other and then try to raise your arm, keeping it straight, against the tension developed. This will help to give flexibility to your muscles.

2.   *Eyes*: you can strengthen your eye muscles by making a deliberate exercise of looking at objects which are at different distances. The change of focus will activate the muscles which control the shape of the lens in your eye. Another exercise is to look out of the right corner of your eye, and then rotate your vision round, upwards, to the left and downwards, keeping the eye as near the edge of the socket as possible. It should be said that these eye exercises are a very minor part of your physical training programme, and need only be practised once in two weeks.

3.   *Back and waist*: another useful exercise is to do press-ups, which will help strengthen arms and will also put your stomach and back muscles into condition. However, your back will need more attention than this alone, and a helpful exercise is to lie on the floor, face downwards, with your arms folded under your chin, palms downwards. Now raise your head and chest from the floor, at the same time trying

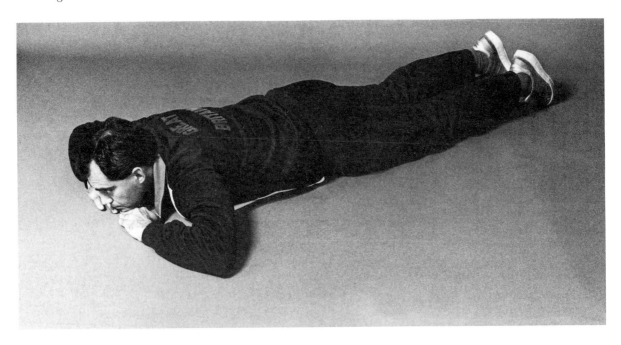

(a)   Lie face downwards with hands under chin.

(b)   Raise chest, arms and legs simultaneously and hold for a few seconds. Gradually extend the duration you hold them up.

114

(c)   A variation is to spread your arms out and back as if you were doing a swallow dive, and hold that position for a few seconds at a time.

to raise your legs. You will not be able to move them far, but hold them up for a few seconds and gradually increase the length of time.

To strengthen your waist, stand with your feet apart and with your arms across your chest so that the fingers touch. Now turn to your left, extending your left arm as you do and try to reach as far round as you can. Then turn to your right, bringing your left arm back to your chest and extending the right arm as you turn. Reach hard round, and back. Really put some effort into reaching as far round as you can, and build up a good swinging rhythm.

Another waist strengthening exercise is to stand with your feet apart and your arms straight down at your sides. Keeping your head up – do not lean forwards – bend over to one side, reaching down with the arm on that side as far as you can, while bringing the other arm up into the armpit. Beat down three or four times in one direction, then come upright and do a similar exercise on the other side. Repeat this for two minutes at a time at the start, gradually extending the time each week.

(a)   Strengthening and loosening the waist: reach down on one side, bringing the opposite arm up under your armpit. Beat down, and really stretch yourself.

(b)   Repeat in the opposite direction. Do not lean forwards. Reach hard down as far as you can, and beat down several times.

(a)   Deep breathing and lung development: stand in fresh air, hands by sides and breathe out forcibly through your mouth.

(b)   Breathe in through your nose, and as you do so turn your palms outwards and raise your arms slightly to help expand your rib-cage fully.

4.   *Breathing*: a good exercise to help develop deep breathing, using the bottom as well as the top part of your lungs, is to stand with feet together, preferably in fresh air, such as before an open window, with your arms straight down at your sides. Breathe in deeply through your nose and, as you do so, rotate your arms outwards and raise them slightly, this will help to expand your rib-cage. Hold this full breath for five seconds and then exhale forcibly through your mouth. Pause, and then breathe in again. Repeat this for two minutes at a time each day.

All these types of exercises can be added together to create one sequence of what was once called 'Swedish drill'. This will help you to complete the full range without forgetting any, as well as establishing an easy rhythm.

There are other useful exercises which can be done at any time of day almost anywhere. You can carry a tennis ball with you and squeeze it from time to time to strengthen your fingers. You can hold your breath, and see how long you can hold it, gradually extending the duration each time.

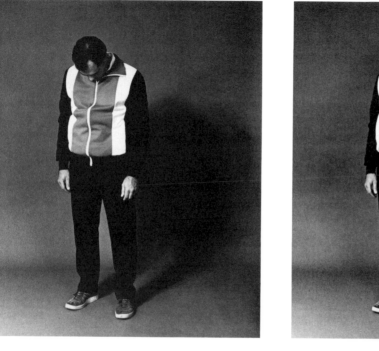

(a) Neck loosening: push your chin into your chest.

(b) Push your head backwards.

(c) Push your head to your right. Do not lean forwards.

(d) Push your head to the left. Staying upright, feel your muscles stretching.

117

DRY TRAINING

Dry training covers the use of your pistol to practise various techniques without firing a shot. It is therefore something you can do in your home and it should be done frequently as a regular item in your training plan.

Remember that a pistol can be damaged if you repeatedly release the striker without a cartridge case in the breech to absorb the blow. Three things can happen:

1. The firing pin can hit the breech and damage both itself and the breech.
2. The point of the firing pin can shatter, due to being stopped without coming into contact with a softer material.
3. The shaft of the firing pin can be damaged by a similar shock. It will hit the inside of the breech block, having come further forward than it would if a cartridge case had stopped the firing pin.

When you do your dry training, engage the dry training mode on your pistol, which allows the trigger to be cocked and released without affecting the firing pin. If your pistol does not have a dry firing capability, you should insert a training cartridge case in the breech – this could be a purpose-made plastic 'round' or a spent case. If you use the latter, remember to change it frequently, otherwise the firing pin will hammer the case to a point where it will cease to be helpful.

You can obtain special training trigger mechanisms for some pistols, such as the Walther OSP, which enable you to fire five successive dry 'shots' from one cocking action in order to practise your rapid-fire trigger release and aiming procedures.

Dry training should be used to practise your trigger control. Take your normal grip on your pistol, paying attention to its finer points to ensure that it is correct and that the right part of your finger is touching the trigger in the appropriate place. Using your normal stance for the speed of rise in the discipline you are practising,

bring your pistol into the aiming position, with proper breath control, and focus on your sight picture. You do not need an aiming mark for this exercise, so you can point the pistol at a blank wall. Concentrate on squeezing the trigger straight to the rear and obtaining a smooth let-off, followed by a steady follow-through. Obviously, without a recoil to disturb the pistol, you can see any fault you may have. Practise this exercise diligently as it will be of great benefit when you come to release a live shot.

Practise trigger control with your eyes closed. This will stimulate your senses and you will be able to visualise your sight picture while releasing your dry shot.

Another exercise which will enable you to keep your pistol steady during an extended aiming process should be carried out in the same way, but this time with a card on the far wall. This card should be black with a small white circle in the middle; the size of the circle will depend on how far the wall is from you and also your ability to hold the pistol steady within a small area of movement. You can use a smaller circle as you progress. Now, when you come on aim, concentrate on maintaining the correct sight picture and on keeping the aim within the white circle as you release the trigger.

You can also do this exercise without squeezing the trigger. Merely practise holding the pistol steady for a considerably longer time than you would take to fire a shot. This will help to develop your muscles, and will augment the benefits of your physical training in a more realistic situation.

A development of this type of exercise is to use a scaled-down miniature target at which you can aim, and so practise a normal let-off, bringing together sighting, aiming, trigger control, breathing and holding steadily. This is not a substitute for the above exercises, but is another one you should practise. You can buy scaled-down targets, or you could make your own.

LIVE TRAINING

No matter how much dry training you do, you will need to carry out a regular planned programme of live training to experience the effect of firing live shots and so build up your confidence. Do not go to the range 'just to practise'. Plan your shooting to achieve a certain objective, just as you have done in your dry training.

One of the first exercises you will need to do is to practise your trigger control. This can best be done by turning the target round and shooting at its plain back. Without the distraction of an aiming mark, you can concentrate on maintaining the correct sight picture while you squeeze the trigger directly to the rear, in line with the fore and aft line of the barrel.

You will find that you can quite accurately judge where the vertical centre line of the target is, but as your hand and pistol obscure the bottom of the target, you have no means of estimating where the horizontal middle line would be. This does not matter, however. You are not shooting for a score, you are practising certain techniques. Thus, your shots will form a vertically elongated group – yet it is surprising how small is the group they do form. Many beginners will shoot a much tighter group when carrying out this practise than they do when they are shooting at a target. There is a lesson there to be learned.

Provided you have maintained the correct sight picture, any shots going outside the group to the sides will most likely be the result of trigger error. Take your grip again and, with great care, place your finger correctly on the trigger. Now make sure you squeeze it straight to the rear, with no side pressure. This exercise

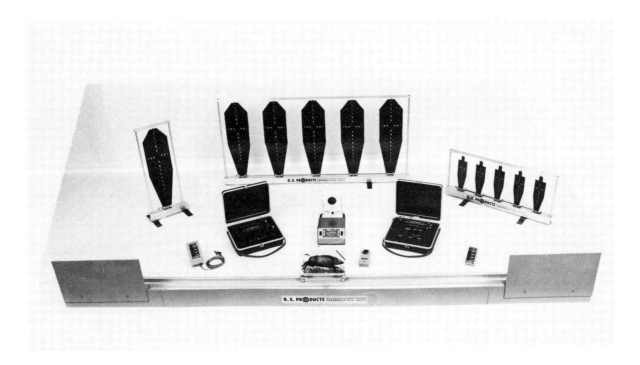

A selection of moving target apparatus made by RX Products which can be used in competition or for training. The bank of five rapid-fire targets on the right are scaled down for use at five metres or ten yards. The Running Boar air rifle apparatus is a good means for air pistol shooters to improve their trigger release.

is strongly recommended as regular practice for *all* shooters throughout their shooting careers. It will sharpen your performance.

A useful exercise is to cut the middle out of a target. At which ring you decide to make this cut will depend upon your shooting ability, but the idea is to put all your well-released shots through the hole. You are not concerned with the good shots. Now any shots hitting the target, that is, going outside the group, show up clearly and you can analyse them to determine why they went where they did.

Some training can become boring and you can obtain relief from this, while still carrying out some constructive practice, by using shooting games. One such game is called 'step shooting'. In this exercise you set yourself steps to achieve which get ever harder. For instance, if your average is 90, you should attempt to score: 90 with ten shots; 45 with five shots; 36 with four shots; 27 with three shots; 18 with two shots; and 9 with one shot. If you shoot a higher score you will be pleased, but it does not affect the game. If you fail to shoot the score required, you revert to the beginning and start again. when you have achieved all the steps, you start again, but raise the score needed by, for example, one point at a time.

If you have a companion whom you can shoot against, you can play a form of tennis. You toss a coin to see who will start. The first person fires one shot. The other person then fires and has to beat or equal it. If he beats the first score he gains a point, and if he equals the score both shooters receive one point. If he fails to beat the first score then the first shooter receives a point. You carry on in this fashion until one shooter has reached seven points with a two-point lead over his rival. One advantage of this live training is that it does bring in an

Peter Stahl conversion kit, shown here fitted to a Colt Government .45, enabling it to fire .22 rim-fire cartridges.

element of competition and you can get the adrenalin flowing.

In order to reduce the cost of live training with a centre-fire pistol, you can obtain spare barrels, slides and magazines which will convert your pistol to a small-bore one. Another method is to buy a conversion unit, such as that marketed by Peters Stahl of West Germany, which will do a rather similar job. When using these .22 conversions, do not neglect to do some training with the full-bore pistol, or you will find the recoil and recovery very different when you come to shoot a match.

If you wish to practise timed-fire and rapid-fire disciplines and have no one to operate the target mechanism, or to time you, you can use a tape recorder to simulate the range officer's commands. Record the words of command and use a stop-watch to allow adequate time for you to load between series. Then blow a whistle to give you the start and stop signals at the appropriate times. Record it at full volume so that you can hear your recorder when you are wearing your ear protectors.

USING A COACH

For a pistol coach to be effective he must establish a good rapport with the shooter. Needless to say the shooter has to have confidence in the coach. This relationship will take time to become established, and while this is happening the coach should be studying his pupil, analysing both personality and shooting results, how those results were obtained and under what conditions. A coach should be very careful not to destroy the relationship which is being created; yet this can easily be done in the early days if the coach jumps to a wrong conclusion in his desire to try to help his pupil.

The coach will need to spend a lot of time watching the pupil shooting. The higher the standard of the shooter, the harder coaching becomes. Basic mistakes are usually fairly obvious and the coach can offer good advice which will have significant results. As the shooter's proficiency increases, it becomes less

easy to see, just by watching, what he may be doing incorrectly. What a coach cannot see is the exact sight picture which the shooter has at the moment of trigger release, yet this could be most useful information.

Happily there is now a training apparatus which does provide this type of information. The Finnish company Noptel has produced a training and analysing system known as the Noptel ST – 1000, which uses a laser beam to indicate exactly where the barrel is pointing. The device is fitted to the pistol and is aimed at a special target. It provides a fast and accurate picture of the whole sighting process and also indicates where the bullet would have struck. This information can be displayed on a television screen and/or stored in a computer and printed out in graphic or diagrammatic form. The computer will store this information for the last 100 shots, and in each case covers the ten seconds before and half-second after trigger release. Unfortunately the Noptel ST – 1000 is quite expensive, but it will be valuable equipment for centres of shooting excellence and for the larger clubs.

A coach will seldom be able to make categoric suggestions to improve your shooting. What he can do is to discuss with you what you are doing during any particular process, to help you analyse your actions, and to show the advantages and disadvantages of alternative methods. The coach cannot fire the shot for you. It is for you to implement the fruits of your discussions.

PSYCHOLOGICAL TRAINING

Once the technical aspects have been mastered, good shooting depends very much on maintaining your concentration for each shot, regardless of the internal and external pressures to which you may be subjected. In this section we will examine some of the techniques that can be used to assist you in realising your true potential.

The Noptel ST–1000 marksmanship training and analysing system, with laser attached to pistol. Note the trace on the visual display unit showing the pistol's movement in the aiming area. To the right is the printer which plots the movement in graphic form.

Mental Approach

Whenever you pick up your pistol (either at home for dry training or at the range for live training) you should have a specific purpose in mind. It is no good saying that you want to score 100. You must analyse your basic techniques (stance, grip, trigger pressure, watching the sight picture, aiming, breathing, trigger release, and follow-through) and train for each specific skill. Similarly with the mental aspect of your shooting: if you get nervous before a competition, it is necessary to train yourself to channel this nervousness into your shooting performance in a *positive* way, by training and experience. You can rehearse the start of a match mentally by imagining yourself going through the whole procedure from arriving at the range, going through weapons control, setting up at the firing point, firing the sighting series and then . . . the *match*! Many people find the first match shot difficult – do not think you are the only person who is nervous.

Anxiety and Fear

In any stressful situation, such as a job interview, an exam or a sporting competition, the body prepares itself for instant reaction to 'danger' by releasing adrenalin to all nerves and muscles – the so-called 'fight or flight' mechanism. In most sportsmen this has a positive effect; but in shooters the effect is almost totally negative. The target shooter has to remain calm and stable (both physically and mentally), relaxed and concentrating on the specific task of firing a correctly released shot and/or series of shots.

Adrenalin causes an increase in the pulse-rate and other physiological reactions such as sweaty palms and butterflies in the stomach. It is therefore necessary to take measures to counteract these negative influences.

Positive Thinking

First, avoid the build-up of anxiety. Anxiety often comes when you are not sure about your ability, and is the product of negative thoughts. Combat this by thinking positively: remember all the hours of training you have done; remember that usually you will shoot a score fairly close to your normal average. If you are competing against top shooters it is perhaps unrealistic to expect to win, so set yourself a realistic goal in terms of your own ability – not someone else's. This is where most shooters, regardless of their ability, gain most satisfaction from shooting. The real competition is solely the individual against himself and his normal standard. If you can enter an important competition, say a regional or national championship, and produce your average performance, one that you would expect on your home range, you can have reason to be pleased with yourself.

If you do not win, it is probably because your average standard is not high enough, so work must be done to improve it. Do not expect too much of yourself. Enter the match with the knowledge that in all probability you will shoot your average, and do not worry about winning or losing – save that for when the last shot has been fired!

Relaxation

Apart from positive thinking, another useful method to adopt before, or even during, a match is relaxation. Unless you are very unusual you will find it difficult to 'switch off' suddenly and relax when in a stressful situation. But this can be done with training. One such method is to sit, or preferably lie, down in a comfortable position and systematically relax all the muscles in your body, starting with your toes and working all the way up your body to your face. Tense one muscle group at a time, and hold it tense for a count of five, then slowly relax it for a count of five. When you have reached your shoulders, move to your fingers, forearms, upper arms, shoulders and finally the face. Imagine your body is made of lead and feel it sinking into the chair or floor. While performing this exercise, try to breathe gently and evenly and gradually slow down your breathing rhythm.

Now that the body is relaxed you can start to relax the mind. It is best to focus on a particular image – such as the sight picture – and concentrate on this to the exclusion of all other thoughts. At first the period of time before your concentration lapses will be relatively short, but with regular practice of as little as ten minutes each day you should find your concentration span improving. This 'imagery' method is also particularly useful if you have trouble sleeping at night, and by using the sight picture as the image, you have the added benefit of building into your subconscious mind a reference point which can be used during competition. In theory, if you can master this method, it is possible to get to the finely tuned state where the mere act of picking up your pistol and looking at the sights automatically reduces the pulse-rate. But even at a less advanced stage, it is an excellent method of relaxing the body controlling the mind in preparation for a competition.

There is another useful relaxation exercise which you should practise if it is to be able to help you before or during a match. You choose an imaginary sanctuary to which you will go when you feel stress taking a hold on you. This mental sanctuary may be a room, or a church or an open space. If it is a room, you must design it in your mind. Will it have windows, or none? What colour will you make the walls? What floor covering will it have? What furniture would you like in it? What can you see out of the windows, if anything? Perhaps you would like to look out on a colourful garden, or have some soothing background music playing. You decide just what your mental sanctuary will be like so that it is tranquil. Perhaps your sanctuary will be in a church, with sunlight shining through stained-glass windows, throwing diffused patterns on the stone floor, while an organ is softly playing in the background. Or maybe your mental sanctuary is an outdoor location, perhaps a tropical beach with the sea lapping on silver sand.

Whatever you choose, make it so that it is comfortable and soothing, and having chosen it, keep to it. Then when you feel stress mounting, sit down, close your eyes and visualise yourself in your sanctuary. Absorb its atmosphere while you breathe gently. After a while you will feel your pulse-rate slowing and all your muscles relaxing, and with them your mind will relax. Now visualise yourself picking up your pistol, loading it, taking up your stance, taking the correct grip, raising your arm and taking aim. See yourself squeezing the trigger straight to the rear, see the foresight being drawn back through the notch in the rear-sight, visualise the trigger release, see the bullet going straight through the middle of the target, and see yourself executing a perfect follow-through. Now open your eyes, stand up, take a deep breath and resume your place on the firing point ready to continue the match.

You must however carry out this mental exercise in training too, practising it frequently for it to become effective in the real situation.

Pre-match Nerves

Everybody has experienced pre-match nerves to some degree, but they have a different effect, depending on the individual's psychological make-up. Some people are able to channel these nerves into something positive like concentration and achieve above-average performance. Others are overcome by nerves and produce below-average results.

There is no easy way to get rid of nerves. Indeed, some degree of nervousness is probably necessary to produce a good performance. But the negative effects can be minimised and the positive effects emphasised by proper preparation.

1. *Planning*: before going to the competition, plan and check everything. Ensure that you know where you are going, how to get there and how long it will take. Be sure to leave yourself plenty of time for setting up at the range (especially if you have never been there before).

Ensure that your equipment is clean, in working order and that you have enough of the right kind of ammunition.

2. *At the range*: before the time for your shooting detail, try to visit the firing point on which you will be shooting. Is there anything unusual about it which might cause you problems? Is there a bench? A chair? Is the target in sunlight or shadow? What about later on, as the sun moves round? Are there a large number of spectators? Feel the atmosphere of the range and imagine yourself on the firing point calm and in control, having considered all of the possible problems and how you are going to handle them. Now you know there are not going to be any nasty surprises that might throw you into a panic.

At this point it is worth repeating that a thorough knowledge of the rules will give you confidence in dealing with any problems that might arise during the match, such as pistol malfunction, target malfunction, disturbance by other competitors, and so forth. Knowing your rights in any particular situation will increase your confidence in being able to cope with any problem.

3. *Mental preparation*: having set up your equipment in good time, with everything in its allotted place, you should prepare yourself for the match. It is vital that you adopt the same

procedures for the match that you normally use in training. Do not do things differently just because it is a match. If a physical warm-up is not part of your normal routine, do not be tempted to copy the person next to you who does have it as part of his routine. If you think it is a good idea and wish to try it then write it down and promise to use it next time you go training – then forget all about it for this match, concentrating on what you are doing and nothing else.

Ideally your match preparation will include:

(a) Physical warm-up exercises (*see* page 128).
(b) Mental warm-up exercises.
(c) Relaxation exercises (*see* page 129).

4. *Mental warm-up exercises*: in the same way as you perform physical warm-up exercises to get the muscles in full working order, it is necessary to warm up mentally prior to starting the match. While sitting on the firing point, and probably after you have performed your relaxation procedure, rehearse your technique for firing a shot or series of shots. Picture yourself with a good stance, taking hold of the gun and taking the correct grip. Imagine loading the gun, breathing properly, and taking aim; feel your finger on the trigger and see the sights still and properly aligned with the target. 'Squeeze' the trigger and follow through. 'Watch' the bullet as it hits the centre of the target. Relax and go through the procedure again, remembering that you are doing everything properly – you are in control and are confident of your ability.

After a few minutes of this rehearsal your official preparation time of ten minutes prior to the start of the match will begin. Now you can pick up your (unloaded) pistol and dry fire. Mould together the perfect elements of your technique from the mental rehearsal with the physical 'reality' of your actually practising those elements.

5. *The sighting series*: sighting shots are obviously important, as they will tell you whether you are sighted in for the particular light (and sometimes wind) conditions of the range. Thus they should be fired as well as you can, and with as good a technique as possible. It is advisable to fire three shots first without 'scoping (but making a mental call if you felt any of them would have been errors). This will ensure that you do not 'chase your shots', that is, make sight alterations based on individual shots, but rather base them on a group.

Remember these shots count for nothing in the match – do not get excited if you fire a perfect group. Conversely, do not be despondent if they are all in the white. The only thing you need from the sighting series is the knowledge that the gun is properly sighted in; then if the sights are correct in relation to the target at the moment the bullet leaves the barrel you will get a good shot.

Some people use the sighting series as practice and in events where an unlimited number of sighting shots is permitted (such as the air pistol and free pistol) fire 20 to 30 shots. This may demonstrate a lack of training and/or confidence. If you are properly trained, have confidence in yourself and have warmed-up properly, there should normally be no need to waste time once the sighting shots have confirmed that the gun is sighted in.

Often you find that nerves disappear quite quickly once the match is under way. General match nerves also disappear with experience. There is a natural progression from being nervous the first time you shoot a competition target on your home range, to the first open meeting you attend, to the first national championship and so forth. As you reach each new step, the first time is hard, but as you become more experienced at that level, the nerves tend to dissipate. Some world-class shooters contend that a shooter may need the experience from over fifty matches before they can reproduce their training scores in matches. Obviously it varies from individual to individual.

Attitude

To have the correct attitude is vital if you are going to succeed in pistol shooting. Remember, you are striving for perfection in the knowledge that it is almost impossible to achieve. However, a good positive attitude, treating each shot as a match in itself, and consistently applying the same technique to each shot, is the best way to give yourself a chance to succeed.

Negative thoughts are no use at all. On the other hand, it does not pay to be too optimistic and unrealistic. It is necessary to strike a balance, which will be determined by the psychological make-up of the shooter and his ability level.

You must always remember, it is a sport – albeit a serious one. It is necessary to be determined and competitive but it is not the end of the world if you have a bad shoot. There are reasons for shooting badly which can be analysed. Faults can be corrected and there will be many more good days in the future. But as we have said before, the main competition is against yourself. You can give yourself the best chance of winning by adhering to a few basic rules, which can be summarised as:

1. Be positive.
2. Be confident.
3. Shoot each shot/series as a match in itself.
4. Analyse what you do and why – and do not be afraid to alter your technique if all else fails.

As we have said, it is vital to have the right attitude if you are going to succeed in any sport – and in shooting, where you are competing in a purely individual way (even if the individual team members' scores are aggregated for a team competition) it is most important.

Some examples of the correct attitude are:

1. *Organise* your training programme, your competition programme, your equipment and yourself!
2. *Thoroughness* in completing your training programme, in your preparation, in cleaning your gun, in fact, in all you do.
3. *Positive thinking*: remember that you are shooting for a total score. One bad shot need not ruin the total; each shot is a match in itself.
4. *Quiet confidence*: if you can exude an air of quiet self-confidence and control it makes you feel better, and your competitors regard you as a threat (if they are thinking about you winning, they cannot be concentrating on their sights).
5. *Seek perfection*: to get a perfect X-ring ten, everything must be correct. Get used to doing everything as well as you can, in your daily life as well as in shooting. But be realistic.
6. *Realism*: do not expect to shoot a ten with every shot. Usually you will shoot your average score – sometimes higher, sometimes lower. Have realistic goals and work methodically towards them.
7. *Dedication*: if you aspire to reach the top level, you must be prepared to make sacrifices in your daily life in order to carry out your training programme fully.
8. *Persistence and determination*: never give up.

SUMMARY

Mentally, competitive shooting is all about confidence. If you can go into a match with the knowledge that you have prepared properly, you can expect to do well.

5 Shooting the Match

PRE-MATCH PREPARATION

Training Programme

An essential part of your match preparation is to ensure that you have carried out your training programme conscientiously. If you have done so, you will gain added confidence from knowing that you have done everything you can to prepare for the approaching match. But, conversely, if you have skipped over some of your training, you will worry that you are not as well prepared as you should be, and this will have a harmful effect upon your morale at the most crucial time.

Equipment

Strip your pistol and clean it thoroughly well before the match, so that you have time to shoot a training session after you have cleaned it and before the match. Never clean a pistol thoroughly immediately before a competition; always shoot it after cleaning, as stripping and cleaning can alter the pistol's characteristics.

You should make a check-list of all the equipment you wish to take, and then you can simply tick off each item as you go through your equipment. You should carry your shooting gear in a box where there is a place for each item, so that you can quickly see that everything is present and in good order. Wind up your stop-watch and run it a little to ensure it is serviceable. Top up your carbide sight blackener with water and calcium carbide.

Ammunition

Make sure you have sufficient ammunition for the match, and allow sufficient for re-shoots due to malfunctions or tie-breaks. Ensure that the ammunition is from the same batch and that you have tested this batch so that you know how it performs. When testing ammunition, including air pistol pellets, shoot them from the pistol you will use in the match. Bullets may perform differently in different pistols, so only test them in the actual gun which is going to use them.

It is a good idea to test your air pistol pellets in a chronograph, to obtain a precise measurement of their speed. Shoot some 20 pellets from each batch, and compare different makes of pellet to see which performs best in your pistol. Look for the smallest divergence from the mean, rather than for the fastest pellets. Remember you are always seeking consistency in pistol shooting to reduce the variable factors.

Rules

Well before the match, you should study the rules and regulations, so that you know exactly what you will have to do, and how and when you are to do it. Carefully reading the rules can actually save you points in a match, and knowing precisely how the match will be run will give you additional confidence. Anything you can do to help reduce worry on the day will reap dividends should stress develop during the match.

Sleep and Diet

Try to get plenty of sleep the night before a match, and, better still, try to get plenty of sleep for a period before that, so that your body is accustomed to this routine. Similarly, maintain a regular diet with plenty of carbohydrates which will provide the body with nourishing food during the run-up to a match. Adjust your daily routine so that you can eat the last meal before the match at least two hours before you start to shoot. You do not want a lot of blood around your stomach digesting your food when you are shooting. If it is not possible to eat your meal two hours before the match, eat only a light meal. Avoid drinks which contain caffeine.

To sustain you during a long match, take a flask of cool (not cold) drink which has an amount of glucose in it. Glucose is easily absorbed into the blood and will provide energy for your nerve cells, so delaying the onset of fatigue. Take frequent sips of this drink to refresh yourself between series. Do not drink only occasional large amounts.

Travel

Plan the time it will take you to reach the range, and allow some leeway for unforeseen delays. You want an unhurried journey to the range, and a leisurely check in.

Weapons Control

Most matches will require you to present your pistol to the official weapons control point where it will be measured, weighed and examined to see that it conforms to the rules laid down for the particular discipline. This should cause you no worries, as you will have taken the precaution of seeing for yourself that your pistol does meet the standards required well before the match. When your pistol has been passed by weapons control, it will usually have a label stuck on it to show that it has been cleared.

Although the limitations on size, overall weight and trigger weight have a small tolerance, it is wise to give yourself a little grace by keeping your pistol well within the limits laid down. It has been known for a measuring box to have swollen due to very humid weather, making it appear that the pistol was larger than it really was.

Warming-up Exercises

When you have booked in and had your pistols approved by weapons control, find a quiet corner and carry out your warming-up exercises. These are intended to loosen your muscles, removing any overnight stiffness, to increase the amount of oxygen in your blood and your level of muscular co-ordination.

Stand with your feet apart, arms at your sides, with palms facing inwards. Breathe in deeply through the nose, rotating your hands outwards and raising them slightly as you do so. Hold this for ten seconds and then breathe out forcefully through the mouth, lowering your arms and turning your palms inwards as you do so. Repeat this exercise five times.

Still with your feet apart and starting with your arms at your sides, rotate your arms in as large a circle as possible. Circle some five times.

Next, loosen your neck muscles by turning your head first to the right and then to the left, five times; then bend it forwards and right back, again for five repetitions.

Now put your forearms horizontally in front of you with palms uppermost, and elbows at your sides. Close your hands. Make circles with your closed hands; first five times clockwise, and then five times anticlockwise.

With your feet apart put your hands on your hips and lean forwards; now rotate your trunk, first to the right, then back, and then to the left. Do this three times, and then repeat in the opposite direction.

Next loosen up all your muscles, by little jumps, while standing on your toes and shaking your arms and fingers as you do so. Just let your body flop about.

Follow this with a short spell of running on the spot. Now start to calm down by repeating the deep breathing exercise with which you started your warming-up session.

Reconnoitre

If possible, visit the range and firing point on which you will be shooting. See if there are likely to be any problems and feel the atmosphere. Check that all the equipment you expect to use at the range is there, such as a chair, a firing bench and side screens. See how sun, shadows and wind may affect your target. Mentally rehearse yourself, firing a shot on that firing point.

Weather and Light Conditions

If you are shooting on an outdoor range, you should have paid attention to the weather forecast. This will ensure you have the right clothing with you for the expected conditions. In addition, it may be possible to choose your own time for shooting, in which case you may be able to select more favourable weather conditions. Nearer to the time to shoot, pay attention to the light, see if clouds are occasionally obscuring the sun, and act accordingly if you are shooting at long range. See from which way the wind is coming and whether or not it is steady or gusting. Plan your shoot for the prevailing conditions.

If you are shooting in a closed range, have a look at the general level of illumination. Stay in the range for some twenty minutes before starting to prepare for your match, so that your eyes become adjusted to the light in there.

SETTING UP

Equipment

Most match rules permit you to set up your equipment on the firing line ten or even fifteen minutes before the time you will start shooting. Take full advantage of this. Set out your equipment in a routine manner. Only have those items you know you will use, or are very likely to use, on the bench, and keep the rest of your equipment near to hand in its carrying case.

One of the first things to do is to blacken your sights, so that your eyes have plenty of time in which to regain their normal vision. Arrange your telescope so that it is focused on the correct target, and so that you can look through it without moving your feet from your firing stance. Have your stop-watch in its correct place so that you can read it easily. Place your sight alteration card, with your 'epsilon' sight picture reminder on it, in front of you so that you can look down at it between shots. Place the screwdriver for adjusting the sights near at hand. If stickers have been issued to be placed on each match target, make sure they will not be blown away. If you need to fix your own target to its frame, place your clips ready for use. Finally, place your magazines and pistol on a soft piece of non-fluffy material in front of your shooting hand, with sufficient ammunition for the match beside them. Make sure you have nothing in front of your pistol which could be damaged should an accident occur while you are loading, unloading, or assuming the 'Ready' position.

Mental Preparation

Once you have set up your equipment, you should prepare yourself for the match. Sit down and breathe quietly and deeply to start with. Each time you exhale, let your body relax. Close your eyes and visualise yourself releasing a perfect shot. Visualise yourself picking up your pistol and loading it, taking your grip on the pistol, assuming your proper stance and adopting the 'Ready' position (if relevant); 'feel' your finger being placed on the trigger, raising the pistol on aim; visualise the correct sight picture, and maintain that picture while you see yourself squeezing the trigger straight to the rear. Visualise the shot breaking and see the sights as you recover and complete the follow-through. 'Watch' the bullet as it hits the centre of the target. Relax and go through the procedure again, remembering that you are doing everything properly – you are in control and are confident in your ability.

After a few minutes of this rehearsal, your official preparation time of ten minutes prior to the start of the match will arrive. Now you may pick up your (unloaded) pistol and dry fire. Mould together the perfect elements of your technique from the mental rehearsal with the physical 'reality' of your actually practising those elements.

In the pre-match period do not look at other competitors' scores. You are not concerned with scores at this moment – yours or other people's. You are concerned only that each shot release will be as near to perfection as you can make it.

SHOOTING THE MATCH

Use of Sighting Series

The sighting series of shots is not in the programme to let you warm up your gun; most important matches will provide two minutes for that prior to the start of the sighting series. The sighting series should be used to make an assessment of the light and other conditions. You should take just as much care in releasing your sighting shots as you do for competition shots. When you have fired three shots carefully, and are satisfied with your call that they were good releases, look through your telescope to see where they have grouped. Decide whether you will need to alter your sights. If you do need to alter them, do not guess at the alteration. Look at your sight adjustment card and make the necessary number of clicks, turning the screw in the direction shown on your card. Many experienced shooters have lost a point from moving their sights in the wrong direction.

It is advisable to fire at least three shots before altering your sights, in order to have a group to assess. If you alter your sights on less, there is a danger of 'chasing your shots', which may occur when you make sight alterations on just one shot.

When you are satisfied that you have centred your group on the target, and you feel your trigger releases were comfortable and well controlled, you are ready to start the competition shots.

Competition Shots

Your training will have been designed to teach you how to fire a perfect release, and now you will apply that training in each of your competition shots. It is paramount that you understand that you are not shooting to create a winning score. In any match you will have succeeded if you obtain your training average. If you shoot a personal best score, you can certainly be very pleased – that will be the jam on the bread! Your mental approach should be one of relaxed self-confidence, a confidence based on knowing you have trained diligently, prepared your equipment thoroughly, studied the rules properly and rehearsed the match mentally.

When you come up on aim for the first shot, your intention must be to release the shot to perfection and that is all that should be in your mind. You should not be thinking about the final score, or about the score this shot is going to make. Think only of the perfect release of the shot that is in the barrel. It follows that if you do release the shot correctly it will hit the middle of the target – but that is incidental to its perfect release. We cannot emphasise too strongly how important it is that you think only of launching correctly the shot that is in the barrel. Do not worry about shots which have already been fired, except in as far as they form a group which may have shifted from the middle of the target; and do not think about shots yet to come. Think only of the one in the barrel; that is the one which your actions are going to affect. It is up to you to ensure that your actions will be correct.

If, at any time, you feel that the release is not proceeding perfectly, for whatever reason, immediately push your finger forward off the trigger, lower the gun and reassess the situation. Then regain your concentration and prepare to fire the shot. Of course, you cannot do this in the rapid-fire events, which is why you must be even more highly trained for these disciplines. In these you get no second chance; your technique must be right the first time and every time.

Once you thoroughly understand that success in pistol shooting will come from applying the technique, and not from straining to fire a perfect score, you will find your scores mounting and your enjoyment growing.

First Match Shot

You have determined from your sighting series that your pistol is sighted in and now you are ready for the competition. Here we must differentiate between, first, those events fired under a

*Paul Leatherdale shooting to win the 1985 British Pistol
Championship (note his good stance).*

Shooting the final of the British Pistol Championship, using spotters to plot the shots for the benefit of spectators, 1986.

strict time limit at the range officer's command (standard pistol and the rapid-fire section of the centre-fire and sport pistol match); second, those fired in the shooter's own time, without much time pressure (precision section of centre fire and sport pistol, air pistol and free pistol); and third, those which are a combination of the previous two types of event, such as the rapid-fire event where the shooter nominates when he is going to shoot (within predetermined limits).

The approach can vary for each of these three situations, as follows:

1. Here the shooter must be committed to fire (apart from calling 'Not ready') as soon as the targets turn to face him. There is no time to think about anything other than the shot.

2. In this situation the shooter has the option to choose whether he wants to fire the shot. If the pistol does not settle properly he can come down and start again. However, this can cause a problem for somebody who is nervous. There is no easy way out other than to concentrate on basics and try not to fire a bad shot. Play the percentages – do not try to achieve perfection, but settle for a nine instead. This will allow you to take the pressure off yourself and get into the match. There is, of course, a limit to the number of times you can afford to do this.

3. In this case the rapid-fire shooter can steady himself and mentally rehearse his first shot several times during his preparation time. But once he has called 'Ready' there is no turning back!

Coaching

If you are shooting as a member of a team it is usual to allow you to be coached during the match. However, normally the rules do not permit your coach to approach you on the firing line. If you wish to speak to your coach you must take the initiative, and leave your position to speak to him. Your coach is there to help you, so do not be slow in asking for his help.

As in other aspects of pistol shooting, if you have not been in the habit of discussing your shooting with a coach, do not start to do it in a match. For good results to stem from coaching there has to be a mutual understanding between coach and shooter and this takes time to be created. Coaching is not permitted in individual matches.

Relaxation

There is an adage 'relax, and success will surely follow' and this certainly applies to pistol shooting. When you are concentrating, it is easy to become too tense and engrossed. Therefore, make a deliberate point of relaxing between each series, or whenever the situation allows. For instance, if there is a malfunction re-shoot, or any other disturbance in which you are not involved, use the time to relax. Sit down, bend forward with your hands on your knees, and breathe deeply. Each time you exhale let your body go limp.

If you find you are becoming over-anxious, you can channel your nervous tension into creating greater concentration by going through a relaxation process.

Sit down and close your eyes and breathe deeply. When you exhale, let your body go limp. Now visualise the 'room' you chose when you began your psychological training, and go into it. Quite soon your pulse will decrease and you will feel your concentration growing. When this happens, whilst still in your mental room, visualise yourself loading your pistol and preparing to fire a perfectly released shot. See yourself taking the correct grip, assuming the right stance, visualise the correct sight picture and then see yourself gently squeezing the trigger straight to the rear. Imagine you are pulling the foresight directly back through the notch in the rearsight. Visualise the shot breaking; you may 'see' the bullet going straight through the middle of the target, and see the follow-through. Now open your eyes, stand up and set yourself up to resume firing.

Sight Alteration

The sighting series should be used to assess where your shots are grouping on the target, so you should alter your sights to centre this group on the scoring rings or zones. But, if you find that there is a consistent error in your shooting *during* the match, do not be afraid of altering your sights to counteract it. There is a psychological barrier against altering the sight, but they are made to be altered – take advantage of this fact. However, you do not want to overdo this to the extent that you are forever altering your sights. If three or four well-released shots have formed a close group you

Trophies won by Paul Leatherdale at the 1987 British Pistol Championships.

Paul Leatherdale receiving the Gallie Memorial Challenge Cup from NSRA Chairman Tony Clark (1984).

can assess if there is a need to alter your sight. If it appears that an alteration could centre this group, then do not delay, as any further shots going into the same position will deprive you of valuable points.

You will know how far one click of your micrometer sight will move a shot on the target at the particular distance at which you are shooting. Write this on your sight alteration card, so that nothing is left to memory or chance. In addition, your sight alteration card will show you in which direction to turn the relevant screw to make the desired alteration. When you alter your sight, write down the alteration you made, so that you can analyse its effect later, and you will be able to judge better what other alteration may be required. With

the information on your sight alteration card, and a record of what alterations you have made, you need have no fear that you are going to upset your pistol. It is simple to turn the sight back to where it was should you wish to do so.

Do not alter your sight on the result of only one or two shots. The minimum information can stem from three shots if they were properly released and called as perfect at the time of their release. More shots will give you a fuller picture, but you risk losing points while the picture is building up.

Rules

During the match there may well come a time when your knowledge of the rules can assist you

Some of the rewards for successful pistol shooting! Prize presentation at the British Pistol Championships, with Frank Leatherdale addressing the winners when he was chairman of the NSRA's Pistol Committee.

and, conversely, where your lack of knowledge could deprive you of points.

For instance, if you call 'Ready' in a rapid-fire series and the targets do not turn to face you within four seconds, this could upset your rhythm. Provided you did not fire when they did eventually face you, you can ask for the procedure to be repeated (UIT *Special Technical Rules*, rule 6.7.h).

The rules have been written to help everyone equally, so do not be afraid of using them. Of course, you may well be afraid of that if you are unsure of the rules, which is why you should study them carefully. Now, in the match, may be the time for you to apply that knowledge to good effect.

Timing Your Actions

While shooting a match, it will help to know how much time you have remaining at any moment. Look at your stop-watch to see how much time has elapsed and deduct that from the time allowed for the match. You may, however, make a simple arithmetic mistake in the heat of the moment, which could make you take some unnecessary action in your panic. You are unlikely to do that in the timed and rapid-fire events, but it does become a real possibility in the events of long duration, such as the free pistol and air pistol events. It can be helpful to have a graph in front of you on which you can plot shots fired against time.

Shooters of all disciplines will derive added confidence from knowing how long it takes to carry out various procedures and actions. Have an idea how long it takes you to do such things as extract an empty cartridge case from the breech, load five rounds into a magazine, walk to and from the toilet, go through your relaxation process or change an air pistol target. For instance, if you are running out of time in an air pistol match, you could decide to fire two shots at one target to save the time taken to change targets. You will know from your knowledge of the rules that there is no penalty for the first two occasions when two shots are fired at one target (UIT *Special Technical Rules*, rule 6.14.a).

CONCLUSION

Good shooting! We will not wish you good luck – luck does not enter into successful pistol shooting. Success comes from knowing and applying the basic techniques, modified as necessary for the discipline being shot, backed up by thorough training and preparation. It is true that we all need good luck at times – but do not rely upon it.

Appendix

SHOOTING AND THE LAW IN GREAT BRITAIN

The Firearm Certificate

In order to possess a firearm in Great Britain you must first have a firearm certificate (or FAC, as it is called for short), as required by the Firearms Act of 1968. This you obtain by application to your local police station. There is a fee to be paid for the first application and for each subsequent renewal. Once granted, the FAC is valid for three years. Usually the police will want you to be a bona fide member of a rifle or pistol club (in club names the two words are synonymous), and they will check with the club's secretary to ensure that you are. You will also be asked to provide the names and addresses of persons who can vouch to your good character. Note that you need an FAC to 'possess' a firearm – this means to buy or borrow, in other words, to have it in your possession.

You also need to have an FAC to possess ammunition. You will be asked to say how much ammunition you wish to be allowed to buy and to have at any one time. Most small-bore ammunition is sold in boxes of 50 rounds, with 500 to an outer box. You may well shoot over 1,000 rounds in the course of three days at a national meeting, and will probably wish to purchase your ammunition in 500-round boxes, so do allow for this when completing your FAC application form. Remember that in addition to the ammunition you want to buy, you will probably still have some of your last purchase in your possession.

Each time you wish to add an item to your FAC it is called a variation, and a renewal fee may be charged. It is as well to cover your likely requirements in the first instance, or when you renew the certificate, to save added expense.

If you wish to use a CO2 pistol this too will need to be entered upon your FAC. Whilst it does not, by law, have to be used only on an officially authorised range (which will have a certificate issued by the Ministry of Defence), it does have to be used only on an 'approved' range. The difference is that an approved range can be set up in, say, a sports hall and does not need the Ministry of Defence to authorise its use for air weapons.

In granting you a firearm certificate the police will want to know how you propose to keep your pistol or pistols and ammunition safely under lock and key when not in use. Steel boxes which can be securely bolted into a cupboard in your home are made for this purpose. Or, of course, a safe can be used.

It is an offence in Great Britain to have a firearm and ammunition for which a firearm certificate is required in a public place without lawful authority or reasonable excuse. Therefore you should always carry your FAC with you. If you do not produce it when asked to do so by a police officer, your pistol and ammunition may be seized. Safeguard your FAC as carefully as you do your pistol as it is a valuable document. Ideally, do not keep the pistol and the certificate in the same place, in case either is stolen.

Minimum Age

In Great Britain there are restrictions on the possession, purchase and acquisition of firearms and ammunition by young people under the age of 17.

Buying and Selling Firearms

You will need a firearm certificate before you can acquire a pistol or ammunition for it. The person from whom you buy your pistol will need to enter the details in your FAC, and in his (as a disposal). Ensure that his authority to sell you the pistol is entered in table 1, column E of your FAC. Similarly, if you sell a pistol to someone, make sure that you enter the number of your FAC in his certificate. In addition, you must write to your chief officer of police to inform him that you have disposed of your pistol. There is no charge for deleting a firearm from a certificate, nor for replacing one with another of similar type, but you must inform the police of the relevant details, including the serial numbers of the weapons involved.

Further Reading

The National Rifle Association of America's *Pistol Rule Book*

The National Small-bore Rifle Association's *Rules and Regulations for Small-bore Rifle and Pistol and Air Weapons Competitions*

The UIT's *General Technical Rules for all Shooting Disciplines*

The UIT's *Special Technical Rules* for pistol events

Useful Addresses

The National Rifle Association of America
1600 Rhode Island Avenue NW
Washington DC 20036
USA

The National Rifle Association
Bisley Camp
Brookwood
Surrey GU24 0NP

The National Small-bore Rifle Association
Lord Roberts House
Bisley Camp
Brookwood
Surrey GU24 0NP

United States Shooting Association
122 Lafayette Avenue
Laurel
Maryland 20707
USA

Union Internationale de Tir (UIT)
Bavariang 21
D – 8000 München 2
West Germany

National Pistol Association
21 The Letchworth Gate Centre
Protea Way
Letchworth
Hertfordshire SG6 1JT

The International Long Range Pistol
   Shooters' Association
16 Southdown Way
Westmoors
Wimborne
Dorset BH22 0PL

The United Kingdom Practical Shooting
   Association
'Thanet'
Park Road
Stoke Poges
Buckinghamshire

The Muzzle Loaders' Association of Great
   Britain
PO Box 217
Newport Pagnell
Buckinghamshire MK16 9YD

Index

142